# SANKOFA (RE)SEARCH MODEL

# SANKOFA (RE)SEARCH MODEL

## (Re)membering, (Re)storing, and (Re) birthing Black Boys and Men

**SANKOFA**

Sankofa is a visual representation of the Akan proverb,
"Se wo were fi na wosanfoka a yenkyi," which translates to
"It is not wrong to go back for that which you have forgotten"

# SANKOFA (RE)SEARCH MODEL

## (Re)membering, (Re)storing, and (Re) birthing Black Boys and Men

**Co-Cyphers**

Lawson Bush, PhD | Edward C. Bush, PhD |
Amiri Mahnzili, PhD

Little Black Book Series

RESEARCH METHODOLOGY, THEORY, AND PRAXIS

Volume 2

Universal Write Publications, LLC
New York, NY

SANKOFA (RE)SEARCH MODEL: (RE)MEMBERING, (RE)STORING, AND (RE)BIRTHING BLACK BOYS AND MEN

Library of Congress Control Number: 2025905449

PRINT: ISBN: 978-1-942774-36-5
eBOOK: ISBN: 978-1-942774-37-2

Printed in the United States of America.

Mailing/Submissions:

Universal Write Publications, LLC
421 8th avenue, Suite 86
New York, NY 10116

Website: UWPBooks.com

This book has been partially supported with a financial grant from SAGE Publishing.

*Sankofa (Re)search Model: (Re)membering, (Re)storing, and (Re) birthing Black Boys and Men* is an important contribution to task of restoring wellness to not only Black Boys and men; it is needed medicine for the wellbeing of Black personhood, familyhood, and peoplehood. Bush, Bush, and Mahnzili have gifted scholars, activists, and practitioners, a special gem. This is a must read.

**Baba Dr. Wade Ifágbemì Sàngódáre Nobles**
Co-Founder and Past President, The ABPsi
Founder and Executive Director, The Institute for the
Advanced Study of Black Family Life & Culture, Inc.
Emeritus, Black Psychology and Africana Studies, SFSU

Firmly grounded in theory and undergirded and informed by ongoing practice, this book is an important and thoughtfully developed contribution, not only to expanding the dialog and discourse of African American Male Theory, but also to Black Studies as a whole. The authors intentionally offer their work as an *invitation, invocation,* and *inquiry.* It is an invitation to collaboratively rethink how we do research in Black Male Studies to achieve healing, liberated and uplifting Black thought and practice in the interests of Black boys and men and the Black community.

**Dr. Maulana Karenga**
Professor and Chair
Department of Africana Studies,
California State University, Long Beach
Senior Fellow, Molefi Kete Asante Institute

# Acknowledgments, Libations, and Prayers

**Offered by Nana Dr. Lawson Bush, V. (the rising SUN of Chief Nii Sowah Aleem Omar Rahmaan)**

*Agoo, Agoo, Agoo*
*Onyankapon*
*Asase Yaa, Nana Adade Kofi, and Nana Obatala*
*Father Lawson Bush, IV, and Momma Anne Catherine, if I call one of you, I call all of you.*
*With permission, I call Ancestors Dr. Asa Hilliard, Dr. Amos Wilson, Dr. Frances Cress Welsing, and Dr. Garrett Duncan; come now. O Creator, Abosom, and Nsamanfo, let my words be your words, producing Holy and Sacred scripture. Infuse the text with liberation and resurrection power. Help me to invoke my inner Baba Dr. Wade Nobles, Baba Dr. Na'im Akbar, Seba Dr. Maulana Karenga, Baba Molefi Asante, and Nana Dr. Salim Faraji. Surround me and the work with the enduring love of the Black women in my life: Queen Mother Catherine Bush, Rev. Dr. Jaleesa Jones-Bush, Rev. LaQuetta Bush-Simmons, Regina Bush-Dean, Christal Shambree-Swift, Dr. Jenise Bush, Nana Afi Enyo (with her comes Sis. Shanga and Sis. Shimeka), Ms. Jill Grayson, Phyllis Jeffers-Coly, Nana Akua Two-Hawks Maat, Dr. Tonia Causey-Bush, Dr. Chioma Bush, Thandiwe Bush, Sis. Rumbie, and the one who protected my legacy, Sis. Dr. Libby Lewis. I give thanks to my F.A.T.H.E.R.S., Babas Cloyed, Q, Eddie, and Ahmses. May the work create a space for my legacy and Sun, Heru Lawson Bush, VI, Okomfo Kwabena Pearson, Tavengwa*

*and Suns, and my future and all our Suns, to shine at their highest potential. Lastly, allow the work to always stand as a testament to my gratitude and the brilliance of Bro. Dr. Serie McDougal, III. Ase, Ameen, and Hallelujah!*

## Offered by Dr. Edward C. Bush

*Through the divine revelation of the Creator, the ancestral wisdom flowing through me, and the unwavering love and support of my wife, children, mother, and siblings, I declare with all authority that this book is a sacred text. It is a vessel of liberation, opening the hearts and minds of all who seek to empower, heal, and free African people through their scholarship. May it inspire them to channel divine purpose and create their own sacred texts, rooted in the indefatigable spirit of our people and guided and possessed by the consciousness of our ancestors.*

## Offered by Dr. Amiri Mahnzili

*To the almighty mother/father creator (Onyankopon) Whom men lean upon and do not fall, take this wine and drink. To Yeye Nature (Asaase Yaa), The sustainer of life who we worship on Thursday, take this wine and drink. To the Gods and Goddess (Abosom) Who guide and protect us, give power wisdom and strength, take this wine and drink. To the ancestors (Nsamanfo) Let my words be your words, let my thoughts be your thoughts, and let my actions be your actions, allowing me to serve you and carry out my purpose, take this wine and drink.*

*To the ancestors (Nsamanfo) who watched over and guided this work: Ramona Rodgers (Grandmother), James Baldwin, John Coltrane, Octavia E. Butler, Ermias Asghedom (Nipsey Hustle), El-hajj Malik El-Shabazz (Malcolm X), Tupac Shakur, Khalid Abdul Muhammed, Kwame Ture, Kwame Nkrumah, Marcus Garvey, Carter G. Woodson, W.E.B. Du Bois, and James Yancey (J. Dilla).*

# Foreword

## Get It From the Ground

It is not just grounding that is important for the Pan-African researcher; it is what the ground allows. Malidoma Somé (1998) tells us that building community is difficult, if not impossible when one has lost contact with *the ground*. The same is true for the researcher. In their case, the ground is the ground of African cultural and intellectual heritage. Without groundedness in African cultural essence, Africana scholars are easily swept away into a network of tides, submitting to the push and pull of dominant trends, rising and withdrawing, the researcher and their landscape shaped by the sheer volume and momentum. The authors of *Sankofa (Re)search Model: (Re)membering, (Re)storing, and (Re)birthing Black Boys and Men* have found occasion, in this present moment, to drop their anchor and ground systematic thinking about Black men and boys in the soil of African epistemology. They put forth a strategy for grounding research in a way that allows the process to more accurately mirror the humanity of African men and boys.

They have contributed to the advancement of Pan-African Studies and Black Men's Studies by providing a way for the posterity; the listening ears of generations to come. As a Zulu proverb states, *Indlel' ibuzwa kwabaphambili*, the way is asked from those who have gone ahead. The authors of this text are frontiersmen who do more than explain the philosophical merits of a research process; they provide guidelines to follow for anyone who wishes to know the being of Black boys and men in various facets of life and how to do so responsibly. By positioning the researcher as a healer, they fundamentally call for a reshaping of the purpose and process of research. They also reposition research as ritual and practice the role of ritual in the research process to make it more aligned with African cultural memory, thus making research a process of restoring balance and harmony. How would your research shift if you knew you were stepping into the role of a healer? In so doing, they integrate traditional African procedures into the research process in a way that enhances Pan-African Studies' research ethics. They have disintegrated the detached school of thought in positivist approaches by applying Martin Luther King Jr.'s philosophy of love to the research process. This emergent philosophy comes along with an important critique of objectivity and neutrality in the research process, which King's love doesn't allow for. Their approach of re-grounding includes reclaiming. The theme of reclamation, which runs throughout the text, includes a rescuing of what is known as the ecological systems approach and relocating it on African philosophical grounds. A particularly important aspect of this text's reclamation is its relocation of the hard sciences. It reunites the hard sciences with spirituality, which is critical to the Sankofic growth of Pan-African Studies and its effort to reclaim the breadth of its intellectual territory.

This text includes a series of practical steps. At this time when there are a plethora of theoretical frameworks, paradigms, and theories designed to understand people of African ancestry, this text authors a highly useful set of criteria for how the researcher should go about matching a framework to their research objective. Furthermore, they guide the researcher in engaging in constant self-interrogation of themselves and their own positionality. The practical steps in this text make the text accessible to the student, professional researchers, and critical thinkers in all pockets of society.

It is my hope that this text will be a part of a larger Sankofic call to Pan-African Studies and Black men's studies to relocate its research approach and purpose on the grounds of African culture(s). The heritage of African histories and cultures represents the ground that is available to us all, that calls upon us all. Let this be the generation that sparks a revival of reaching into that soil to situate its research on African epistemic grounds because it is this grounding that will allow for a renaissance of new approaches, methodological tools, theories, and approaches that reflect more accurately who African people and what African people want to echo Marcus Garvey. As I mentioned, it isn't just grounding; it's what grounding allows. Somé's warning was that building is hard without grounding, so let the ground beneath our feet as researchers be African. For the gymnast, it is the ground that allows them to push off, land precisely, and perform spectacular feats, flips, and jumps; it is the launching point where an Olympic pole vaulter plants their pole, transforming speed and momentum into vertical elevation. The authors have provided a generation of readers with a process they may use to guide their intellectual curiosity about Black men and boys, transforming it into intellectual and practical energy to elevate African people. Their process draws power from the solid foundation of African cultural essence in which they planted their inquiry—and they get it from the ground.

Serie McDougal, III, PhD

Professor, Department of Pan-African Studies

California State University, Los Angeles

## REFERENCE

Somé, M. (1998). *The healing wisdom of Africa*. New York: Penguin Putnam Inc.

# Contents

# CHAPTER 1

## *Introduction: What is the Role of a Researcher of Black Boys and Men?*

We were grateful to be asked to contribute to the Little Black Book Series (LBBS) on liberatory methodology or methodologies for Africana Studies because of our extensive and ongoing theoretical and direct work concerning and engaging Black boys and men. Indeed, a research methodology for this unique population is a natural progression of the totality of our work and will be deeply rooted in both African American Male Theory (AMMT) and years of African-centered programming and organization building for Black boys and men such as the African American Male Education Network and Development (A²MEND) organization; our rites-of-passage experiences; mentoring—in fact, one of the co-authors is a longtime mentee of the lead author; and taking young men to Africa just to note a few examples of our direct engagement. With this in mind, the purpose and goal of this book are no different from those of our previous and current endeavors. They seamlessly align with the overarching mission of the series, which is to produce mdw ntr or divine words—pure, free, and decolonized Black thought, that we see as scripture and actions that liberate African people, particularly Black boys and men, causing them/us to reach their/our highest level of freedom and divinity.

To be clear, research and its methodologies share the aforementioned goals and trajectory for us. Researchers cannot meet these aims or travel down this path without thoroughly interrogating and answering two questions: (a) "What is my role as a researcher of Black boys and men?" and (b) "Who are Black boys and men to me?" It is nonsensical and useless to embark on conversations about the utility and appropriateness of such models as positivist, interpretive, critical, or other paradigms without free Black thought and the liberation and divinity of a people as the foundation and focus of one's research.

For the latter, rooting the book in African American Male Theory (AAMT; Bush & Bush, 2013a, 2013b, 2018), which is outlined in Chapter 2, will facilitate the emergence of a new socially and culturally aligned research methodology and aid in decolonizing existing methodologies and critiquing the most commonly used frameworks to research Black boys and men, such as Critical Race Theory. Moreover, among other significant contributions, AAMT challenges deficit epistemologies and approaches to perceiving, framing, and researching Black boys and men. We provide examples of deficit thinking and provide readers with the tools to push past such pejorative approaches, including challenging how researchers and scholars commonly frame their work concerning Black boys and men as being *counter*, that is, counternarrative, counter-storytelling, and the like as a perpetuation of deficit thinking. Counter-storytelling is a method of telling the stories of historically excluded groups as a way to interrupt and stand in opposition to mainstream narratives and stories (Merriweather Hunn et al., 2006; Solorzano & Yosso, 2002). This practice inadvertently links the origin and location of the narratives of African American boys and men to oppression and oppressors. The story of Africans worldwide, including the stories of Black boys and men, who are the original beings along with Black women, on the planet by far, is not counter to any story; it just is.

With respect to the former question, our answer anchors us firmly in free Black thought. In doing so, we position and delineate the role of the pedagogue in the ancient world as being the same role of a researcher, that is, to heal. Nonetheless, the fact that a significant number of researchers are teachers today supports us making the appellation of teacher and researcher synonymous and using them interchangeably.

Using African philosophy, Clement of Alexandria (150 AD–215 AD) writes, "As, then, for those of us who are diseased in the body a physician is required, so also those who are diseased in soul require a pædagogue to cure our maladies" (Clement of Alexandria, 2015). Indeed, much of the world, from antiquity to present, understands that the teaching and learning process is a spiritual and sacred endeavor. The secular schooling system, for the most part, is a very recent and limited phenomenon worldwide. Education has been mostly under the jurisdiction and care of religious institutions, such as temples, mosques, and churches, and has been administered by spiritual leaders and attendants, such as shamans, priests, imams, monks, nuns, Sunday school teachers, and the like for the act of healing. To this end, Hilliard (1997) writes, speaking of African peoples, that "our educational and socialization process was always situated in a sacred space. This space served to clarify purpose and emphasize the divine nature of the process" (p. 10).

Drawing on the oldest complete book in history, *The Teachings of Ptahhotep: The Oldest Book in the World* (Ptahhotep et al., 1987), Hilliard (1997) provides additional insight concerning the role of the teacher–researcher–healer. The ancient text is based on the writings of Ptahhotep, an African sage and scribe, who lived circa 2,350 B.C.E. His 37 short teachings were called wisdom text by some but were understood by the Africans of the Nile Valley, to be mdw ntr or divine words.

Hilliard (1997) cites the following paragraph from *The Teachings of Ptahhotep* that illuminates the role of a teacher then he follows it as we do below, with his analysis of the text:

> May your servant be authorized to use the status that old age affords to teach the hearers, so as to tell them the words of those who have listened to the ways of our ancestors, and those who have listened to the gods.
>
> May I do this for you so that strife may be banned from among our people, and so that the two shores may serve you.

Hilliard's analysis:

1. The scribe, Ptahhotep, requires God's permission to teach. Therefore, teaching is a spiritual task, divinely sanctioned.
2. Experience is the high qualification.
3. Teaching is for hearers (a prepared, ready, receptive, focused student).
4. The teacher teaches the words of the ones who listened to the ancestral ways, and the one who listened to the Gods. (This is a spiritual and cultural curriculum, the essential content of education. It goes far beyond mere preparation for a job.)
5. One aim of the teaching is to eliminate strife among the people to bring harmony to bring order.
6. The second aim is so that the two shores, east and West banks of the Hapi (Nile, metaphorically east and West Bank refers to the matters of life and death, respectively), may serve God. (Maybe in the likeness of Ra, may together be one with God, in purpose, in behavior.) (p. 72)

Extrapolating from ancient wisdom outlined by Ptahhotep and Hilliard, the role of a researcher of Black boys and men is clear. To operate in this compacity, you must see yourself in the likeness of God and that the post or position of researcher was ordained and sanctioned by God so that you can produce divine research. This is achieved by a keen ability to listen or be a hearer of your participants, your wise ancestors, and God. The goal of your divine endeavor is to eliminate strife caused by falsehoods. Thus, the researcher is a healer. To conduct research that will liberate and inspire the divinity of Black boys and men, the overarching function and position of the researcher must be that of a healer who constantly seeks God and the permission of God to carry out this divine charge.

Yet, in addition to looking at ancient narratives to answer the question of what is the role of a researcher of Black boys and men, the term research itself provides an answer that is rooted in pure Black thought and praxis. The usage of the prefix *re* is particularly interesting. Would not the word *search*, meaning to examine thoroughly to find something or someone, be sufficient to describe what we ascribe to the word research, the simplest definition of which is a search for the truth? According to Dictionary.com, re is "a prefix, occurring originally in loanwords from Latin, used with the meaning 'again' or 'again and again' to indicate repetition, or with the meaning '*back*' or '*backward*' to indicate withdrawal or *backward motion*" (emphasis ours). Thus, in this light, one can define *(re)search* as the process of going backward, again and again, to search for or find the truth. This emergent view of research parallels the Akan concept of Sankofa, meaning to "go back and fetch it," symbolized by a bird with its head turned backward while its feet are facing forward, holding an egg in its mouth. Operationalized in the diaspora, Sankofa takes on the meaning of using one's history as a guide to move forward. We contend that Sankofa is more than a construct or a symbol; it is also a spirit. We are saying that a (re)searcher of Black boys and men must operate in the spirit of, or be possessed by, the spirit of Sankofa to produce divine words or narratives to heal Black boys and men.

Under the Sankofa (Healer) (Re)search Model, to (re)search is to be relentless and indefatigable, to go back and search again and again for the truth. This kind of pursuit or search may push the researcher beyond the boundaries of Westernized training and quantitative and qualitative empirical measurement tools because studying Black boys and men is a complex, multifaceted, multidimensional, and cosmic and in motion phenomenon. This framework has the following three overlapping, nonlinear, and bidirectional yet distinctive components that the researcher of Black boys and men must embody and employ, which are to (re)member, (re)store, and (re)birth. To (re)member is the act of gathering the dismembered. Black boys and men, in the context and environment of white hegemony, exist in a dismembered state well beyond love. Researchers must gather the fragmented parts of the data, history, and body of literature, looking past the dominant pejorative narratives of Black boys and men to make them/us whole again as a process of (re)membering. To (re)store is to resurrect Black boys and men. After (re)membering, it is the power of the researcher's words; this is the view that researchers aim to produce scripture, divine words, through positioning, analyzing, and theorizing in ways that breathes life and (re)stores. To (re)birth is to use the Sankofa (re)search approach, the act of looking and going back again and again as a guide to create or recreate or to birth or (re)birth new and free paradigms, language, and meaning as an act of worldmaking.

This three-prong approach is not new to Black thought and consciousness as it is captured in the following ancient African trinity story of Ausar, Auset, and Heru.

*The Deity Ausar was the king of Kemet, and his reign was marked by love and respect from his subjects. However, jealousy festered in his brother, Set, who harbored ambitions of seizing Ausar's throne. One night Set snuck into Ausar's room and measured his body. Afterwards, he commissioned a beautiful chest to be made adorned with vibrant paint and gold sheets. Later, at a grand party, Set presented the chest as a challenge, claiming it would belong to whoever could fit perfectly inside. Set convinced Ausar to try the chest, which sealed him within as planned. The chest containing Ausar was cast into the Nile by Set and his accomplices.*

*Ausar's wife, Auset, was devastated. She searched for and found the chest, recovered Ausar's lifeless body, and concealed it in river grass. Furious, Set cut Ausar's body into fourteen pieces. To make sure that the body was never found again, he hurled the pieces all over Kemet. The next morning, Auset returned to the river with her sister and friends, to perform the necessary rituals, only to find Ausar's body gone. Auset transformed into a huge bird and flew high over Kemet to search for Ausar. Using her sharp vision, she was able to find all his pieces, and she (re) membered his body.*

*On the night of the full moon, Auset employed magical words to resurrect Ausar.*

*Auset (re)stored Ausar to life by breathing the breath of life into his body, and shortly afterward, they conceived a child. Grateful, Ausar explained that having died, he needed to reign in the after-life. Before departing, he assured Auset that she would bear their son, Heru, who was destined to defeat Set. After Heru's birth (or rebirth), he was hidden and protected from Set by his mother. At the appointed time, Heru fought Set in a fierce battle. Heru triumphed over Set, although he lost his left eye in the battle. The eye, known as the Wadjet, later became a symbol of healing. Heru became the king, and order was (re)stored to Kemet.*

While there are many versions of the above narrative, the basic components are that Ausar was murdered by his brother Set, cut into pieces, and scattered throughout the Nile Valley. Ausar's wife, Auset, *(re)searches* all over for him. She eventually finds all the *members* of his body and *(re)members* him. Auset then uses her divine words to *(re)store* or resurrect Ausar to his full spiritual God-self and consciousness. Not only that, from an African ontological and epistemological perspective—free Black thought, we are the past, present, future, that is, the yet-to-be-born, the living, and the after-living (Nobles, 2023). Thus, Auset *(re)births* Ausar, the lord of the dead and (re)birth, in the form of Heru as a divine healer and leader.

See Figure 1.1 for a pictorial representation of the Sankofa (Re) search Model that we will also call the Sankofic (Re)search Model. The general standard approach to decide whether to include a figure in your work centers mostly on clarity, relevance, and enhancement of the written text (American Psychological Association, 2020). When deciding whether to add a figure (or table) to research, consider the following guidelines:

1. Relevance: Is the figure or table essential to understanding the research?
2. Clarity and Enhancement: Does it clarify or illustrate a point better than text alone?
3. Redundancy: Does it duplicate information already presented in the text?
4. Quality: Is the figure clear, legible, and well-designed?
5. Purpose: Does it support the research question, hypothesis, or conclusions?
6. Space: Figures can help conserve space in the main body of the text, especially when presenting large amounts of data.

While we recommend these guidelines, we do not contend that Figure 1.1 adheres to them. We have other motives and rationales that we want you to think about as you consider a research paradigm for Black boys and men that is anchored in pure Black

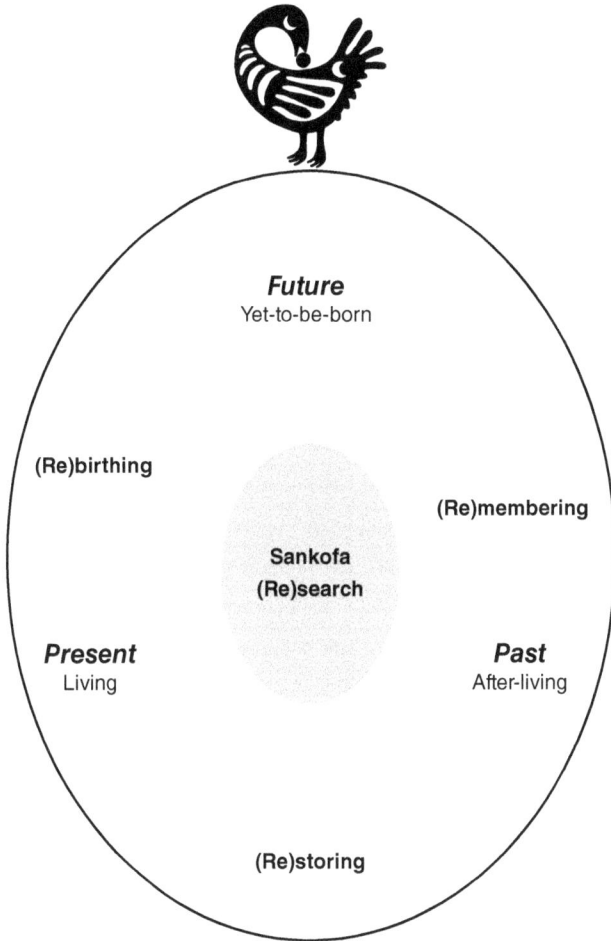

**Figure 1.1** Sankofa (Re)search Model

thought with healing in mind. We are aware of the power of symbols to leave an indelible imprint on the psyche, mind, and spirit. Moreover, African signs and symbols hold deep meanings and significance in African spirituality and culture, representing beliefs, values, and stories passed down through generations. They are often used to invoke blessings, protect against negative forces, and communicate with the spiritual realm. For example, the vèvè are mystical and esoteric sketches, traced upon the ground, walls, and on all sorts of objects, designed to focalize the energies of specific spirits. The drawings or figures aim to create an environment where spirits are more likely to manifest themselves by taking physical form. Essentially, the vèvè can be considered as the distinctive signature of the Gods (Rigaud, 1969). Other examples include the Ankh symbol for eternal life, the Eye of Heru (*Wadjet*) mentioned before for protection of the Kemetic people, the motifs of Adire of the Yorubas "are created, accepted, and standardized aspect of the people's culture, are drawn from history, legends, myths, proverbs, folklores and deep observation of the environment of this traditionally deeply religious people" (Areo & Kalilu, 2013, p. 22), and the Adinkra symbols of the Akans (Marfo et al., 2011) like the Sankofa symbol used in our figure to invoke the value, and spirit of (re)search, (re)membrance, healing, and forward progress.

The egg is the dominant image in Figure 1.1, as there is one in the mouth of the Sankofa bird. In various African cultures and cosmologies, the egg can carry diverse symbolic meanings, often representing aspects of life, fertility, regeneration, spiritual transformation, and creation. In the Yoruba creation story, it is said that Olodumare sent down an egg to the primordial waters of existence. This egg contained the potential for all living things and was seen as the origin of creation. The cracking or hatching of the egg is associated with the emergence of the first divine beings, known as the Orishas. Thus, the concept of the egg represents the primordial state from which the universe and life originated.

With Figure 1.1: Sankofa (Re)search Model, we are saying one must go back, again and again, to the primordial state at the intersecting possibilities of the past, present, and future, where (re)membering, (re)storing, and (re)birthing exist in a perpetually symbiotic, dynamic, and seamless state, to move forward and heal. Taken altogether, our figure not only serves as a practical guide to conduct (re)search, but it also simultaneously serves as an invitation and invocation for the (re)searcher of Black boys and men to be enveloped in the spirit of Sankofa.

Given the explicit direction, position, and agency of this current text, a reasonable question might emerge for the reader, even if what we have presented thus far resonates with you, that is, "shouldn't researchers be neutral and objective?" Let us pause here for you to answer that question along with thinking about the following ones: Is it possible for researchers to be neutral and objective? And has research about Black people been neutral and objective?

We want you to continue to think about the question of should researchers be neutral and objective as you proceed because this question is tied to the overarching focus of this chapter: what is the role of a researcher, particularly of Black boys and men? The question of neutrality is also connected to the methodological concept of trustworthiness, that is, the degree to which one can find a study credible, generalizable, and dependable. We discuss the latter aspect of the question later in the text.

In thinking about whether it is possible for researchers to be neutral and objective, let us consider the classic work of critical theorist Paulo Freire (1993), *The Pedagogy of the Oppressed*. He makes the case that no part of the educational enterprise is apolitical or neutral in that it either supports the current asymmetrical power structure and hegemony or it does not. This line of thought falls under critical research, one of the three main models of research approaches; positivist is equated to quantitative analysis and interpretive is associated with qualitative inquiry are the other two. Critical research, inextricably linked with critical theory, refers to an approach to research that goes beyond describing and explaining phenomena. It aims to uncover underlying power structures, ideologies, and social inequalities, questioning established norms and challenging dominant perspectives and the notion of the neutrality of research and researchers. It is from the view of the non-neutrality of research that researchers began to explicitly state their positions in their work. A positionality statement is most often placed in the introductions of dissertations and research papers for authors to reveal their ontological and epistemological assumptions. Positionality is shaped by researchers' subconscious and conscious beliefs and values along with their racial and gender identities, political allegiance, line of work, religious constructs, geographical location, upbringing, social class, and the like. Moreover, it influences every aspect of the research process including the overall research approach, types of questions asked, and the analysis of data, findings, and conclusions drawn (Cohen et al., 2002; Foote & Gau Bartell, 2011; Grix, 2018).

In the last chapter, we will discuss more about the importance of writing a positionality statement, which is a soul-searching Sankofic process; yet, we hope that our entire work forces you to grapple with your positionality. The path to producing mdw ntr or divine words—pure, free, and decolonized Black thought, which liberates African people, particularly Black boys and men, causing them/us to reach their/our highest level of freedom and divinity, is through you. In other words, the Sankofic approach requires the researcher to be willing to go through the process of (re)searching, (re)membering, (re)storing, and (re)birthing oneself. Nevertheless, our objective in discussing positionality and critical research at this juncture is to bring out and encourage your engagement with the possibility, and perhaps the reality that all researchers inherently come from a position and carry an agenda. In fact, a researcher's program is commonly referred to as a *research agenda*. Within the academic realm, scholars are often expected to introduce themselves by presenting their research agenda. This perspective emphasizes that researchers, by nature, cannot be entirely neutral or objective. Henceforth, the response to the inquiry of whether research on Black individuals has been impartial and objective should be "no." The African story of Ausar, Auset, and Heru is instructive here to help us understand the historical approach of the research aimed toward Black people worldwide. The aspect of nature in the form of Set best characterizes the role of research in the lives of Africans in that his function was to dismember Ausar and to spread his truth or body so far that it could never be (re)membered. The classic works *The Mismeasure of Man* (1981) and *Even the Rat was White* (1976) and then the later *works The White Architects of Black Education: Ideology and Power in America, 1865–1954* (2001) and *SKH: From Black Psychology to the Science of Being* (2023) thoroughly demonstrate the non-neutrality of research in just about every discipline and area of study, chief among them being anthropology, psychology and psychometrics, sociology, education, history, theology, medicine, and biology. The explicit aim of the robust body of research, or the so-called research as many of the early studies were based on manipulated and fabricated data to say the least, was to dismember by dehumanization. Nobles (2023) writes that in 2021 the American Psychological Association (APA) offered an apology

> decrying that body's complicit role in perpetuating white racism in society. It was stated that the American Psychological Association was complicit in contributing to the systematic inequalities, and hurt many through racism, racial discrimination, and denigration of people of color. Apologizing for being complicit in harming, undermining, and damaging the health and well-being of persons of African ancestry (both historically and contemporarily) is unacceptable. (p. 20)

While unequivocal examples of how research was used to dehumanize Black people in general and those even specific to Black men are abound, we chose not to rehash these gory details. We as researchers struggled with this decision. On the one hand, we understand that the truth must come to light concerning the magnitude of the efforts to dismember Black bodies using what was passed off as purely objective scientific research. Yet, on the other hand we wonder about the deleterious impact of retailing these stories over and over. We drew upon the indisputable work of Steele's (1997, 1998, 2011) stereotype threat, among other things, to help us in this decision. He makes the case that when members of historically excluded populations are presented with well-known stereotypes about their group, it has a profound negative impact on outcomes, performance, and behaviors. In other words, lies that are repeated often enough must situate somewhere in the mind as truth as some point. We refer you to the four aforementioned texts if you are not aware of the history and proliferation of scientific racism.

As a sidebar, it is important for us to insert here the following paragraph and commentary, before continuing our discussion about the profound responsibility researchers have in deciding what to include in their work based on how one sees their role.

> *Because of the current location of Black boys and men within an oppressive system of white hegemony, and the placement of our Sankofic (Re)search Model in such close proximity to discussions of scientific racism, it may appear that our approach emerges in response to these pejorative conditions. Nothing could be further from the truth. It is not in opposition or a response to these current conditions and milieu; instead, it is a representation of unadulterated, archetypal, and ongoing Black praxis. The constructs that underpin and outline our Sankofic (Re)search Model were developed by African peoples as free Black thought a few thousand years before systems of white inferiority came to inhabit structures of government, education, religion, and economics. (Re)searching, (re)membering, (re)storing, and (re)birthing is how African people responded to the challenges of their own nature in nature to arrive again at their divinity. This paradigm is useful to deal with the Set within and outside of us, in good and bad times.*

We hope that our transparency about our struggle in the decision not to include the horrific details of how science was used to dismember Black bodies is of some use to you. It should demonstrate the weight and responsibility of a researcher of Black boys and men. Minimally, like other healers, your creed must also be "to do no harm." We are not suggesting that other scholars who have testified to the violence inflected on Black bodies were wrong;

Our reflections, prayers, and focus of this work guided us in this direction. Yet, our dilemma begs the following question for you: How do or will you make decisions about what data remain on the floor as you are the ultimate editor of your work? The lead author for the current text shares the following story to help you continue to think about this question.

*I have never forgotten this moment, though it happened over 30 years ago when I was a doctoral student. One of my professors received a research grant to conduct research on Black teachers, and I was hired by her to help collect data. I spent a year, two semesters, conducting observations in the elementary school classroom of a highly seasoned Black teacher. Simultaneously, I was taking an ethnographic research methodology course with the same professor. Whatever data I collected while working for her could be used for my papers in the course.*

*I visited the teacher's classroom twice a week for a few hours. This was in the mid-90s, the height of an African conscious movement, and African-centered education was a significant part of the educational discourse. So, I viewed her classroom through this lens. I developed a complex data collection and coding scheme as I began to make the case for how this Black teacher was failing to implement African-centered education or deal with race, even when ripe opportunities became available. I turned in my paper at the end of the semester.*

*My teacher stated that my work was by far the best paper in the course. I continued to conduct observations and develop my paper. At the end of the year, I was in my professor's office discussing my work and the possibilities of working towards a publication. The discussion along these lines abruptly ended when she stated firmly: "You are not going to publish that paper; there is enough negative research on Black teachers out there!" This was a wake-up call. I had never really thought about my role as a researcher, particularly as an African in this world. I have not stopped thinking about my role ever since.*

*Many years later, while serving as a committee member for a dissertation defense, I shared my story with a student. The student conducted research on the experiences of Black women in higher educational leadership. In all of the interviews except one, the Black women talked about how Black men had been helpful in their development or ascension as leaders and that white women had been more than adversarial and hurtful. The one dissenting narrative characterized white women as being helpful and said that Black men were the opposite. The student offered no analysis of these divergent findings.*

*After sharing my story, I told her that as a researcher, she needed to at least point out this difference and perhaps provide some discussion as to why. However, I pushed further and talked to her about her duties as a Black researcher, telling her that it was her responsibility not to leave Black men out there with so much negative being said, particularly with data in front of her that painted a much different picture of Black men.*

## TOP OF FORM

We hope that these examples help underscore what we cannot stress enough. Though the outcomes of studies are influenced by multiple factors, you, the researcher, are by far the most significant variable. The type of study you choose is mostly insignificant in comparison. To our point, the early scholars in all the disciplines mentioned above used various methodologies and had the same results and conclusions. Driven by the same inferiority complex, they decided that Africans were inferior in all aspects of life and produced research tantamount to their beliefs.

Thus, a great portion of our current text focuses on you with the aim of having you examine your explicit, internal, and latent ontological and epistemological constructs about your positionality in relationship to yourself. This involves an examination of the nature of your own being and how you view, engage, and research Black boys and men. The questions offered at the end of this chapter are designed to do just that.

Moreover, the questions and this book's content are positioned to challenge and engage both the novice and the experienced researcher. In fact, we conclude this chapter with an excerpt from Asa Hilliard's book, *African Power: Affirming African Indigenous Socialization in the Face of Culture Wars* (2002). He outlines what it takes to be a master teacher of African people. With great liberty, we substituted or added to the word "teacher" with "(re)searcher" and changed a few other minor words for flow; nonetheless, focus your attention on the thought of what it takes to be a master (re)searcher of Black boys and men.

African (re)searchers strive for mastery in what they do. As revered figures in the community, they are expected by their communities to do so. Most, if not all, adults are teacher–(re) searchers but the "Sesh" or "Sba" in ancient Kemet (Egypt), the "Jegna" in Ethiopia and the "Jeli" in West Africa, are some of the titles for the master teacher–(re)searchers. These are the (re) searchers who meet criteria for excellence. Most of the following qualifications can be found among African masters everywhere. Though they may be called by other names, the special description of the "Jegna" below is shared with African masters throughout Africa and the diaspora.

- They have been tested in struggle or battle.
- They show extraordinary and unusual fearlessness.
- They produce exceptionally high-quality work.
- They show diligence and determination to our people in everything that is done.
- They vowed to protect, with their lives, their people, land, and culture.
- THEY ALWAYS SPEAK THE TRUTH. (Hilliard, 2002, pp. 18–19)

# EXERCISES AND QUESTIONS

Gather five research articles about Black boys and men. If you are an experienced researcher, you should include your own work.

- Looking back on your past research, or looking at other papers if you are a novice, what was your role or the role of the researcher in comparison with what we outlined in this chapter?
- How did you or the researcher situate Black boys and men?
- Looking at the conceptual/theoretical frameworks, research questions, methods, findings, and discussions, how might the perspectives in this chapter changed those studies' approaches and outcomes?
- How does the chapter expand your conceptualization of yourself and your role as a researcher?
- What is the role of a researcher of Black boys and men?

# CHAPTER 2
## Who are Black Boys and Men to Me?

Building upon the introspection and question introduced in the opening chapter "What is the Role of a Researcher of Black Boys and Men," in this chapter we explore the essential query of how you perceive and position them. This leads to a natural extension of the initial question posed in the first chapter: Who, indeed, are Black boys and men to you? The two questions together profoundly control the research agenda and outcomes in this area of study.

Everyone has a belief or theory about Black boys and men for why they are as you perceive them to be that is deeply influenced by being dismembered by every apparatus and mechanism of society and your personal experiences. No researcher, Black or other, novice or expert, should conduct research of Black boys and men, without a deep self or guided interrogation about their internal assumptions. Thus, we begin this chapter with some pre-chapter work. First, see the questions below that will help you get started on this necessary, and what should be an ongoing, process and undertaking. Second, we want you to begin to think about how you define success for Black boys and men; we have an exercise and question designed for that purpose. Last, we have another exercise that will help you to recognize and develop free Black thought called the Hunter and the Lion. If you are an instructor of research methods, the questions and exercises are great for class discussions and group work. If you are a dissertation chair, insist that your student engages the below. If you are working and reading independently as a student or researcher, do not skip the exercises and questions. Yes, it is a lot of work; but it is work necessary to becoming a Sankofic (re)searcher producing divine words—pure, free, and decolonized Black thought, causing Black boys and men, to reach their highest level of freedom and divinity.

After completing the pre-chapter work, we discuss the function of theoretical and conceptual frameworks in research manu-scripts and provide you with guidelines and an approach to selecting appropriate frames for researching Black boys and men. Next, we cover the significant social and political move-ments that have deeply influenced Black Men's Studies. This precedes examining the body of literature, constructs, and devel-opments that have profoundly shaped the field. Both presentations serve as necessary building blocks for constructing a theory and developing a research model focused on Black boys and men.

Subsequently, we proceed to deconstruct and contextualize the most widely used theoretical framework for studying Black boys, followed by a reclaiming of ecological system's theory. In the final segment, we present the tenets of AAMT and conclude with a discussion that will guide us back to the pre-chapter exercises of this current chapter.

## PRE-CHAPTER 2 ASSIGNMENTS

Who are Black Boys and Men to You?

- What do you really think of Black men?
- Black men are what … Because?
- Where and how did you learn about Black men, and what did you learn?

- What trauma, if any, have you experienced that may influence how you see Black men?
- List three to five assumptions that explain the collective status of Black men today.
- How do you think your answers above influence your research of Black boys and men?

## Defining Success for Black Boys and Men

Google Black men in prison, click on images from the google menu bar, and look at several of the pictures.

Google Black men in college, click on images from the google menu bar, and look at several of the pictures.

- Now answer the following question about which Black man is more successful: Davonte, who dropped out of school because, among other things, he could never sit still in class, "sags," code switches between slang and Ebonics, and is in and out of jail, or William, who speaks "perfect" English, is clean-cut, and has several degrees and a well-paying job at a Fortune 500 company?
- Write how you feel about Davonte compared with how you feel about William.

## The Lion and the Hunter

Close your eyes and picture a lion for about a minute as you conjure up all the characteristics and attributes, real or Disney imagined, about him.

- Write a short list of the adjectives, sayings, and thoughts you have about him.

Now imagine that this lion was captured by a hunter and was put in the hunter's classroom to learn. As you think about the lion in the hunter's classroom, answer the following questions:

- What kind of behaviors would you see from the lion in the classroom?
- What behaviors would you need to see from the lion if you want him to be successful?
- What outcomes would you hope to see, particularly if you wanted the lion **to remain a lion and to be free**?
- Write a short poem praising the success of the lion based on how you have defined it.

## THEORETICAL AND CONCEPTUAL FRAMEWORKS

In general, everyone has a theory about various aspects of life, behavior, and events. In short, a theory is a comprehensive understanding of thoughts and concepts created to interpret, explain, or even predict phenomena to offer an understanding of complex concepts. A theory should advance our understanding and knowledge of particular circumstances, occurrences, and phenomena. Theories should be testable over time and, perhaps, over space and population.

A theoretical framework developed from theory should be used to create research questions, analyze the literature review, formulate hypotheses, and interpret data and results. Typically, the theoretical framework appears early in the manuscript in social and physical science articles. In social science dissertations, the theoretical framework is most commonly in chapter 1; however, it is sometimes placed as part of the literature review in chapter 2. By articulating the theoretical foundation at the outset, researchers establish a clear framework that shapes their study's subsequent exploration and interpretation.

In contrast to a theoretical framework, typically grounded in established and verified theories, a conceptual framework provides a systematic and organized collection of concepts derived from prominent thinkers and ideas within a specific field of study.

However, its location and obligation in manuscripts follow the same guidelines as the theoretical framework. It most often appears in the introductions of manuscripts. Also, it outlines the key constructs, variables, and relationships relevant to a specific study and serves as the foundation for designing, conducting, and analyzing research. Theory is composed of concepts; thus, conceptual frameworks help the development of theory and theoretical frameworks.

In general, to select and develop a theoretical or conceptual framework, researchers should ask the following questions:

- Is the framework a product of your analysis of the key theories or concepts previously explored in your research field?
- Does the framework align with and contribute to your research topic's latest theoretical or conceptual insights?
- Does the theoretical or conceptual framework exhibit a logical, coherent, and analytical structure that supports your data analysis?
- Does the framework enable the analysis of relationships among the variables and ideas in your research?
- Does the theoretical or conceptual framework address how you intend to answer your research questions or test your hypotheses?

McDougal's *Research Methods in Africana Studies* (2017) provides an extensive list and introduction of the various theories and conceptual frames typically used to analyze Black people throughout the diaspora. Some examples include African Womanism, Black Queer Theory, Two Cradle Theory, and Africana Critical Theory. However, even with existing frameworks commonly utilized in examining Black lives, our Sankofa (Re)search Model requires additional questions to the above list when selecting theoretical or conceptual frames for Black boys and men.

- What is the origin of the theory, and when and how was it applied to Black boys and men?
- What is the end goal or aim of the conceptual or theoretical framework?
- How is the framework defining the person—the ontology of Black boys and men?
- Does the conceptual and theoretical framework help explain who Black boys and men are or just what has happened to them?
- Do the frames represent pure and free Black thought?
- Is the theoretical or conceptual framework developed in response to pain or oppression?
- Does the theoretical or conceptual framework account for Black boy's and men's gender and race?
- How is Black masculinity positioned?

## INTRODUCTION TO AAMT

After more than 40 years of research, no uniform theory had emerged as a foundation and frame that explained the lives of African American boys and men until AAMT in 2013. AMMT is now the framework used in a few hundred studies, books, articles, and organizations such as A²MEND. Prior to AAMT, a significant number of studies and other scholarly writings concerning African American boys and men can be characterized as having no explicitly stated theoretical framework. There had been some attempts at theory, for example, Majors and Billson's (1993) *cool pose* framework, which has led to an emergent discussion around a theory of Black masculine literacies (Kirkland & Jackson, 2009; Tatum, 2005). Yet, these efforts gained little traction in this area of study and are specifically focused on groups or segments under certain conditions within the general population of African American boys.

The preponderance of social science literature, particularly in the educational body of research, draws upon Critical Race Theory (CRT) to demystify and encapsulate the lives of African American boys and men (Donnor, 2005; G. Duncan, 2002; Howard, 2008; Lopez-Perry, 2023; Lynn, 2006; Singer, 2005; Stinson, 2008; Watkins & McGowan, 2023). In addition, there are even more studies that though CRT is not cited directly, it is implicit in the frame (Cox Edmondson, 2009; Fenning & Rose, 2007; Kirton & Rogers, 2023; Marraccini et al., 2023; Maylor, 2009; Noguera, 2003; Perillo et al., 2023; Skiba, 2002; Wood & Turner, 2011). While we categorically affirm the necessity of considering racism, power, and cultural hegemony as a framework to analyze and situate this population, drawing on CRT as the sole theory offers a myopic viewpoint and provides a limited foundation on which to build.

## THE STUDY OF AFRICAN AMERICAN MEN AND BOYS AND SOCIAL AND POLITICAL MOVEMENTS

The broader field of Adult Development is a recent occurrence barely in adolescence. Similarly, the study of men is in its infancy, beginning in the early 1970s. Men, specifically white males, have always been highlighted in history for their conquests, but not until the last 50 years have, they been examined regarding their sex-role development, masculinities, and specific male experiences.

There were several major contributors to the early general study of men (see Brod, 1987; Connell, 1995; Franklin, 1984; Kimmel, 1987, 1995; Pleck & Pleck, 1980; Pleck, 1981). Yet, perhaps of greater influence on this particular field was the political and social milieu of the early epoch of male studies. Pleck and Pleck (1980) have contended that there were three social movements that engendered the study of male sex-roles and altered definitions of manhood and masculinity: the women's movement, the gay liberation movement, and the men's movement. However, Franklin (1984) added the moral majority movement as a fourth. The current authors add, specifically in the case of African American men, the Black Power and Civil Rights Movements as a fifth. We also add as a more recent impact on African American male studies and issues, the African-centered Movement as a sixth and, as an ongoing and current impact, hip-hop culture as a seventh.

Not unlike many Black women's discontent with the women's movement (see Cannon, 1988; hooks, 1981), African American males have not been largely involved in the men's movement and others such as gay liberation movement and moral majority movements because many feel that they have little or no relevance for the lives of African American men (Franklin, 1994). This is not saying that African American men's masculinity is not in some ways similar to white men's masculinity in the United States. However, there are some distinctive constructs that were and are produced by very different political, historical, social, spiritual, and economic experiences (Bush, 1999; Jackson, 1997).

Some (Franklin, 1984; Poussaint, 1982) argue that African American males were not recognized as men by wider society until the late 1960s.[1] They asserted that Malcolm X and the

---

[1]Some scholars argue that African American men have been collectively emasculated because: (a) slavery caused a situation where many African American men could not protect themselves or their families; (b) a "matriarchal system" within African American communities caused by an absent father or an "overpowering African American woman" emerged within the context of a patriarchal US society that expects men to be the heads of households; and (c) economic oppression rendered African American men unable to provide for their families in a society where manhood and the provider role are inextricable (see author; Staples, 1978; also see hooks, 1981 for a counterargument).

Black Power Movement created a more assertive and self-confident African American male. This notion was articulated by Ossie Davis in his eulogy of Malcolm X saying that Malcolm X was the embodiment of Black manhood. Consequently, and logically, *men* cannot be studied as men until they reach manhood. Therefore, if African American males did not become recognized as men until the mid- to late 1960s, then the Black Power Movement along with the Civil Rights Movement, which also produced more assertive African American men, must be seen by scholars as one of the major modern movements influencing definitions of Black masculinity and the study of African American men.

The African-centered Movement that emerged during the early 1980s reached an apex around 1995 with the Million Man March, which also influenced Black masculinity and the study of African American boys and men. Baker-Fletcher (1996) credits the African-centered Movement for engendering a *new male* or what he calls an Xodus male. "An Xodus man is one who closely contributes educational, spiritual, and material resources to the community. He values the outer community he lives in because he is so attuned to the inner Community of Self" (p. 25).

Studies published during this epoch (see Hunter & Davis, 1992; Roberts, 1994; Watts, 1993) found that African American males perceived themselves as not fitting the traditional or Western paradigm of masculinity (i.e., aggressiveness, competitiveness, adventurer, provider, and superiority to females). Roberts (1994) concluded from his interviews that African American males are not comfortable with the socially defined traditional masculine ideal. Hunter and Davis (1992) found that African American men's definitions of masculinity clustered around self-determination and accountability, family, pride, spirituality, and humanism. In short, the conclusions drawn from these studies are symmetrical with the African-centered notions of men and women that recognize the "duality or the interrelationship of masculine and feminine experiences in both men and women. African American males are expected to contain in their sex-role identities a masculine and feminine self" (Roberts, 1994, p. 385; see also Akbar, 1991; Karenga, 1980; Nobles, 1980).

Whether the influence of hip-hop on African American boys and men is pejorative or positive is contested terrain. Nevertheless, the influence of hip-hop worldwide is undeniable (Alim et al., 2009). Certainly, its impact on the lives of African American men and boys is far reaching, influencing the speech, vocabulary, dress, and the overall disposition, personality, *pose,* or *swagga* of many African American boys and men, which in most cases depicts a brash assertiveness and self-confidence (C. Duncan, 2010).

Though hip-hop has been around for over 50 years, the study of hip-hop is virtually new, taking firm root over the last 15–20 years. Thus, our perspective on this major social and political movement on African American boys and men in terms of scholarly inquiry is a fragmented picture at best and must be developed and thoroughly investigated in the future of Black Men Studies (Noguera, 2003). Nevertheless, in 2012 the *Journal of Hip Hop Studies* emerged as scholars are well on their way to constructing a more complete picture. Scholars have found that it has an effect on such matters as student learning and engagement, counseling, identity, justice, and racial resistance (Alim, 2006; Anyiwo et al., 2022; Chaney & Mincey, 2014; C. Duncan, 2010; Hicks Tafari, 2018; Klatskin, 2018; Morrell & Duncan-Andrade, 2002; Richardson, 2006; Washington, 2018).

## SUMMARY OF THE BODY OF LITERATURE AND THE STUDY OF AFRICAN AMERICAN BOYS AND MEN

During the aforementioned social and political movements, the literature on African American boys and men over the last 50 years has grown tremendously in terms of both the number of studies and books published and the variety of subjects studied. Over time, there have been some shifts in the body of literature. The early literature positioned African American boys and men more as the objects of study whereas in more recent years they have been more the subject of inquiries. However, irrespective of time periods or the positioning of African American males in research, the study of African American males and the phenomena that contribute to their presumed dysfunction or less-than-desirable social, political, and economic outcomes dominate the literature, though there has been in the last decade or so an additional focus on *successful* African American boys particularly in the educational body of literature (Bonner, 2010; Byfield, 2008; Grantham, 2004; Hrabowski et al., 1998; Kumah-Abiwu, 2022; Warren, 2021; Whiting, 2009; Wright, 2018).

While the early literature concerning African American males dealt with the challenges they faced in society (Grier & Cobbs, 1968; Hare, 1971; Moynihan, 1965; Staples, 1978), a more disturbing but necessary trend surfaced in the body of literature in the mid-1980s that would permeate and profoundly impact the study of African American males. Scholars and others during this era began to systematically compile and report statistics concerning life outcomes for African American males in comparison with other racial and gender groups looking chiefly at homicide, incarceration, life expectancy, and infant mortality rates in which they found that African American males were not only at the bottom of these indicators but that they also outdistanced their counterparts by dramatic and devastating measurements.

The work of Gibbs (1984, 1988), Kunjufu, (1984, 1985), and Madhubuti (1990) fundamentally changed the approach to the study of African American boys and men as they ushered in the *endangered species* analogy and discourse to both the scholarly and mainstream body of literature to characterize the dismal life circumstances of this population: In fact, almost all the subsequent academic and popular literature and educational and social programming related to African American boys and men are inextricably linked to their work. Writers, scholarly or other, after this point were expected to advance the *endangered species* discussion and report data concerning the status of African American males. From the late 1980s and the mid-1990s scholars worked feverishly to compile a mountain of growing pejorative statistics into four categories: (a) demographical and statistical issues; (b) psychological, social, and health issues; (c) political and economic issues; and (d) educational issues (Gordon et al., 1994).

Also, during this epoch there were several important firsts, many of which were described by Majors and Gordon (1994). The early 1990s produced the *Journal of African American Male Studies*, the first academic journal in the United States for African American males. In addition, several research centers were founded. In 1988, the Albany State Center for the Study of the Black Male was established, the first center in the United States dedicated to the study of African American boys and men. Several commissions, committees, and forums were convened to address African American male issues. In 1989, Ohio's governor formed the Governor's Commission on Socially Disadvantaged Black Males, also the first of its kind in the United States. Last, several all-Black male academies and classes began in the late 1980s and 1990s located mainly in Detroit, Milwaukee, and New Orleans, employing mostly all-Black male instructors (Holland, 1991).

More currently, we see a continuation of the type of programing coming out of the 1990s aimed at Black boys such as the My Brother's Keeper initiative launched by President Barack Obama in 2014. The primary objective of the initiative is to tackle enduring opportunity disparities encountered by young men of color and guarantee that every young person has the opportunity to realize their full potential.

In terms of scholarly writings and research, there are no areas of African American males' lives that are off limits to academic inquiry: McDougal's (2020a) book *Black Men's Studies: Black Manhood and Masculinities in the US Context* is a testament to this fact. He covers and examines every subject imaginable concerning Black boys and men. In addition to a host of other books, edited editions, several important themed journal issues have been published during this period in *Urban Education* (2003), *Teacher College Record* (2006), *American Behavioral Scientist* (2008), *Race, Ethnicity and Education* (2011), *Research on Social Work Practice* (2012), *School Psychology Review* (2023), and *Journal of Multicultural Counseling and Development* (2023). Journals have been created such as the *Journal of African American Men*,[2] *Journal of African American Males in Education*, *Spectrum: A Journal on Black Men*, and *Journal of Black Masculinity* to house this expanding body of literature.

While the points of inquiry and the opportunity to publish results have dramatically increased, and even though there has been some movement away from such deficient-sounding language as *endangered*, the central focus of the body of literature about African American boys and men still follows the trajectory of the endangered species discourse in that it illuminates the many social, educational, political, and economic disparities and challenges of African American boys and men.

Moving forward, two influential works shape the field of Black Men Studies: the first being AAMT, and the second, Curry's (2017) book *The Man-Not: Race, Class, Genre, and the Dilemmas of Black Manhood*. In 2013, the field witnessed the emergence of the first comprehensive theory regarding Black boys and men. AAMT delineates the position and trajectory of African American boys and men in society, drawing on and

---

[2]Now it is the *Journal of African American Studies*.

accounting for pre- and post-enslavement experiences. It captures their spiritual, psychological, biological, social, educational development, and station. AAMT gives the field the ability to stand on its own two feet, representing free Black thought.

Curry's (2017) work suggests a conceptual shift, encouraging us to perceive the Black male not as an aspiring participant in white male power but as a victim oppressed by his gender. His work acts as a corrective, offering a framework that challenges prevailing narratives depicting Black men and boys seeking the power of their white oppressors—a narrative pervasive across academic disciplines and popular spaces. Curry contends that Black men grapple with issues such as death, suicide, abuse, and rape, highlighting the need for a comprehensive examination and theoretical understanding of their gendered existence. Curry's latter argument points out one of the shortcomings of CRT in framing the gendered lives of Black boys and men.

## THE PROBLEMATICS OF CRT AND SIMILAR FRAMEWORKS

CRT had its genesis in legal scholarship and discourse (Bell, 1992; Crenshaw et al., 1995; Delgado, 1995); though, we see the works of such scholars like Woodson (1933/1990) and Du Bois (1903/1969) as having great impact on its theoretical origins. Since the introduction of CRT to the educational body of literature (see Ladson-Billings & Tate, 1995), it has been the principal theoretical framework employed by scholars to examine the lives of African American boys and men. Scholars utilize CRT to, among other things, illuminate the under academic achievement, over punishment, state of being beyond love, and the harmful outcomes of wrongfully held stereotypes and perceptions (G. Duncan, 2002; Howard, 2008; Lopez-Perry, 2023; Lynn, 2006; Reynolds, 2010; Singer, 2005; Stinson, 2008; Watkins & McGowan, 2023).

In short, Critical race theorists posit that race and racism are entrenched in every aspect, apparatus, foundation, structure, and function of society mediating both individual and institutional consciousness, policy, and practice. CRT allows one to:

> a) foreground race and racism in the curriculum; b) challenge the traditional paradigms, methods, texts, and separate discourse on race, gender, and class by showing how these social constructs intersect to affect communities of color; c) focus on the racial-ized and gendered experiences of communities of color; d) offer a liberatory and transformative method when examining racial, gender, and class discrimination; and e) use the transdisciplinary knowledge and methodological base of ethnic studies, women's studies, sociology, history, and the law to better understand the various forms of discrimination. (Smith-Maddox & Solórzano, 2002, pp. 68–69)

We wholeheartedly affirm and adhere to the tenets of CRT; yet, we find it to be limiting and myopic in that far too much credit is given to racism and oppression for producing outcomes. Using CRT solely to understand African American boys and men in America, particularly in how it has been used in social science research and epistemology, albeit mostly unintentionally, is like giving a mechanical juicer credit for producing and creating the oranges, the orange trees, and the juice. It would be nonsensical to many, in this metaphor, for one to study the juicer and expect to know much about the orange or the juice. It may be the case that studying the juice provides a significant amount of informa-tion; however, analyzing the juice as if its origins began with an encounter with a juicer is negligent because the juice was already in the orange and thus the juicer is a factor in the production of the juice rather than the reason for its creation or existence.

We equate the mechanical juicer to racism, oppression, enslave-ment, and CRT and liken the outcomes and behaviors of African

American males to being the juice in the aforementioned metaphor. Under the paradigm of CRT and other related theories
including oppositional theory (see Fordham & Ogbu, 1986;
Ogbu, 1987) and the *cool pose* framework (Majors & Billson,
1993) what African American males *do* such as *acting cool*
becomes a reactionary response, suggesting that African males in
America would not be *cool* if it had not been for white cultural
hegemony. For example, Connor (1995) has contended that
*coolness* for African American males help them deal with the
stress caused by social oppression and was developed because
they were not allowed to exhibit conventional expressions of
masculinity and manhood. Colloquially speaking to debunk this
notion, one would just need to travel throughout the African
continent and diaspora to find African boys and men wherever
they are posturing and striking cool poses. Moreover, if they are
observed during ancient rites-of-passages and other traditional
spiritual rituals practiced since before colonialism to present,
coolness can be observed regardless and independent of racism
and oppression.

Whether readers concur with our attempt to debunk the asser-
tion that coolness for African American boys and men is a recent
and localized phenomenon caused by racism and oppression is
not paramount; rather, we aim to convey the necessity of viewing
the experiences of this population from a much broader perspective and thereby calling for a much broader theoretical and
analytical approach than CRT. W.E.B. Du Bois in his book *The
Negro Family* (1909) wrote that "There is a distinct nexus
between Africa and America [referring to Africans and African
Americans] which, though broken and perverted, is nevertheless
not to be neglected by the careful student" (p. 9). To this end,
scholars have long studied the cultural continuity and continuation of African cultural, spiritual, and social practices in the
Americas (Fortes, 1967; Herskovits, 1959; Kenyatta, 1983;

McAdoo, 1988; Nobles, 1980; Sudarkasa, 1980). CRT does not allow such an examination. We are not only acutely concerned with the impact of racism on African American males, we are also interested in a framework that allows one to juxtapose several factors and account for more robust questions.

## ECOLOGICAL SYSTEMS THEORY

According to many indigenous peoples around the world (see Cajete, 1994; Ming-Dao, 1986; Somé, 1994), the universe is made up of a series of interconnected organisms and systems. Likewise, human beings exist in a symbiotic and bidirectional relationship with one another, their environment, and other phenomena. These ancient concepts constitute the foundation of systems and ecological thinking. The current authors view, incorporate, and employ ecological systems theory from the perspective that it is a modern coining and rendition of an African philosophy and ontology (Asante, 1980/2003, 1990; Asante & Mazama, 2005; Jackson & Sears, 1992; Mazama, 2001). In this light, ecological systems thinking is African thought and practice; thus, we find it, among other salient reasons, to be a natural and suitable framework to be the major underpinning of a comprehensive theory for African American boys and men.

Urie Bronfenbrenner is the contemporary progenitor of ecological systems theory. He writes that ecological systems theory offers "a unified but highly differentiated conceptual scheme for describing and interrelating structures and processes in both the immediate and more remote environment as it shapes the course of human development" (Bronfenbrenner, 1979, p. 11). Moreover, it provides the necessary space to account for the environmental influences on human development by positioning individuals, in this case African American boys and men, within a system of dynamic and multidirectional relationships influenced by multiple dimensions and aspects of the surrounding milieu. Similarly with respect to approach, it calls for the investigation of phenomena, events, individuals from a multidisciplinary and transdisciplinary perspective.

Bronfenbrenner (1979, 1986, 1989, 2005) divided the components of the theory into five interconnected environmental systems that include the microsystem, mesosystem, exosystem, macrosystem, and the chronosystem. The microsystem captures the individual's own biology, personality, beliefs and perceptions, and intellectual gifts and the interactions with familial, home, peer groups, neighborhood, and school environments. The mesosystem makes the links between the environments of the microsystem. It is the space where microsystems engage one another; for example, it is the connection between home and school, family and peer groups, and the like. Exosystems are external environmental settings and community factors, such as a parent's place of employment, that impact an individual even if that person is not a direct participant. The macrosystem looks at larger cultures or systems, which can be physical, emotional, and ideological that may affect individual development. These may include regional and national culture and economic and political culture. The chronosystem considers the pattern and arrangement of the environmental events and transitions and the sociohistorical context in which they occur over time such as the change in career opportunities for women over the last few decades (Santrock, 2008).

Using Bronfenbrenner's theory as a foundation and skeleton, it is our aim to move toward a comprehensive approach to understanding the lives of African American boys and men. It is important to note that others, across disciplines, though they have not created a theory from Bronfenbrenner's for African American males, have found ecological systems theory useful in its current state as a framework for this population (Williams,

2009; Woods et al., 2006). Moreover, Jonathan and Cinawendela (2006), theorizing about the impact of such factors as violence, fatherlessness, racism, and poverty on African American boys, were forthright in their call for the need to study African American boys from an ecological perspective. They wrote that the "disproportionate rates of incarceration, poverty, and school failure all speak to the need for a holistic approach to understanding and addressing the problems that these young boys face ... Thus, an ecological, or structural, approach is warranted" (p. 213).

## A COMPREHENSIVE THEORY FOR AFRICAN AMERICAN MEN AND BOYS

In the following pages, we outline the components of AAMT. Our work should be seen as being more nascent than exhaustive; yet, comprehensive and focused enough to provide future scholars, researchers, and practitioners with a viable framework to use and expand upon. The tenets and assumptions of AAMT are that:

a.   *The individual and collective experiences, behaviors, outcomes, events, phenomena, and trajectory of African American boys' and men's lives are best analyzed using an ecological systems approach.*

Building upon what happens in nature, an ancient and current African worldview, and Bronfenbrenner's work, AAMT suggests that African American boys and men exist in a symbiotic and bidirectional relationship with other beings, matter, concepts, and phenomena. Thus, AAMT provides the conceptual framework and scheme to describe and analyze the interrelated structures, systems, and processes that occur in these dynamic and multidimensional environments that influence and shape the development, experiences, outcomes, and trajectory of African American boys and men. Given that the factors in environments impacting African American boys and men are possibly numerous and vastly differentiated, a multidisciplinary and transdisciplinary approach becomes necessary to AAMT.

AAMT incorporates all five of Bronfenbrenner's (1986, 1989, 2005) interconnected environmental systems that include the microsystem, mesosystem, exosystem, macrosystem, and the chronosystem (see the above and Figure 2.1 for an explanation of these five systems). However, AAMT divides the microsystem into two categories: inner microsystem to capture components such as a person's biology, personality, and perceptions and beliefs while the outer microsystem provides the space to analyze the impact of such aspects as the family, peers, neighborhood, and school environments. Also, AAMT expands the mesosystem to show the links between the environments of the inner microsystem, outer microsystem, and a sixth division and system added by AAMT called the *subsystem*.

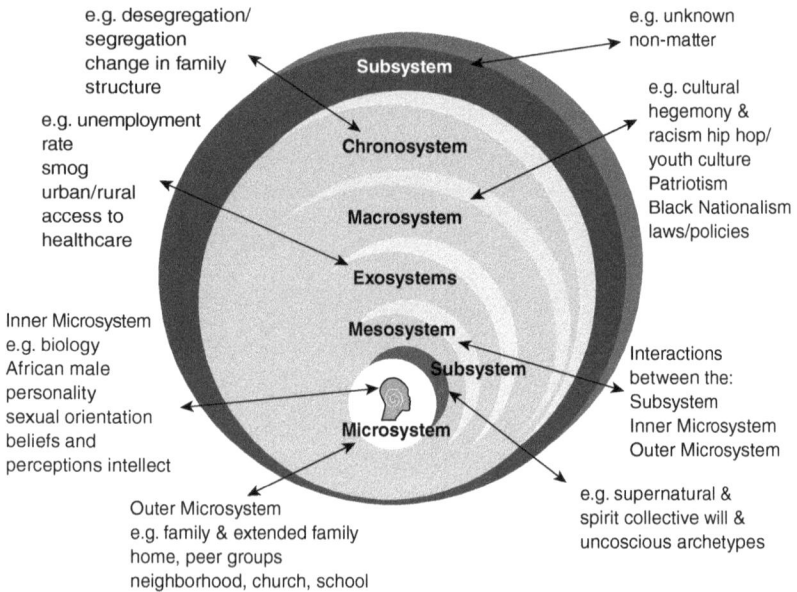

**Figure 2.1**   African American Male Ecological Systems Model for African American Male Theory

The subsystem provides the space to consider the influence and involvement of such matters as the supernatural and spirit (Cajete, 1994; Somé, 1994), the collective will, collective unconscious, and archetypes (Jung, 1968; Taub-Bynum, 1984). Also, it provides the opportunity to consider what renowned and highly regarded physicists describe as multidimensional levels of reality existing in parallel spaces (Kaku, 2005) on the individual male in the microsystem level and as an undercurrent of the other systems in the model. Moreover, the subsystem represents the unknown or what has yet to be accounted for or explained. There is still much to be known and studied as Singh (2003) reminds us:

> One of the key scientific findings of modern times is that the amount of observable matter in the universe constitutes a very small fraction (less than 1 to 10 percent) of the total energy of the universe, while 90% or more of the universe exists in the form of un-manifested dark matter or dark energy. If science believes this finding of its own and takes it to heart, it would focus its investigations and spend its valuable resources on investigating the non-matter based reality. (p. 11)

With this in mind, we are not out to prove in this current work that the aforementioned phenomena exist and that they the affect the experiences of African American boys and men; rather, our aim is to build a theory that is elastic and robust enough to grow and to accommodate the physical and social scientists who currently research such phenomena. In addition, spirituality and the related are important to a significant number of African American boys and men (Baker-Fletcher, 1996; Watts, 1993). The subsystem coupled with the microsystem offers the framework to examine and account for these phenomena via the perspective and narrative of this population.

b.  *There is something unique about being male and of African descent.*

Whether it stems from nature, nurture, or other, there is something unique about being male and of African descent. While AAMT affirms the uniqueness in other populations and groups and is categorically interested in what makes African American males similar to others, AAMT is also concerned with examining and discovering what is distinctive about this population as group and individual distinctions within the group. Distinctions are necessary across areas and disciplines, for example, to create specialized programs, pedagogies, and curricula in education, to focus on specific medical and psychological treatment in biological and psychological research, and to account for the contributions of African American men to forward progress of humanity in history.

c.   *There is a continuity and continuation of African culture, consciousness, and biology that influence the experiences of African American boys and men.*

AAMT asserts that the study of African American men and boys must be anchored in Africa (Franklin, 1994; Harris & Ferguson, 2010; White & Cones, 1999) because there is a persistence of African culture and consciousness that impact African American boys and men (Fortes, 1967; Herskovits, 1959; Hill, 1997; Kenyatta, 1983; McAdoo, 1988; Nobles, 1980; Sudarkasa, 1980). The study of the extent of such links requires multidisciplinary and transdisciplinary approaches as the implications of possible connections permeate the physical and social sciences and humanities. Research on African American boys and men that does not account for the impact of Africa in America runs a significant risk of producing incomplete and faulty assumptions and results. There is much work that needs to be done in this area, inasmuch as most research on African American boys and men makes no attempt to empirically examine or even theorize about the ramifications of such cultural, biological, and spiritual links and continuation.

d.   *African American boys and men are resilient and resistant.*

AAMT posits that African American boys and men are born with an innate desire for self-determination and with an unlimited capacity for morality and intelligence. AAMT embraces resilience theory and vehemently opposes deficit paradigms, thinking, and practice. From this viewpoint, social and educational challenges facing this group stem from socially constructed systems rather than any innate biological or cultural deficiencies. Moreover, Black masculinity is viewed as inherently good, serving as a potent, attractive energy, sharpening tool, and a force to create space for others to move freely as their authentic selves.

Resilience theory meshes well with AAMT as it was first introduced by ecologist C.S. Holling in 1973 who, like the current authors, synthesized aspects of systems theory and ecological theory to construct his work. In short, resilience theory is concerned with and addresses the ability, capacity, and powers that people or systems exhibit that allow them to rise above adversity (Holling, 1973; see also McCubbin et al., 1998). AAMT is particularly interested in discovering and illuminating the resiliency present in the inner microsystem (e.g., biology, personality, sexual orientation, beliefs and perceptions, and intellect), the outer microsystem (e.g., family, extended family, home, peer groups, neighborhood, and church), the subsystem (e.g., supernatural, spirit, collective will, unconscious, and archetypes), and mesosystem (e.g., interactions between the subsystem, the inner microsystem, and the outer microsystem).

In addition, AAMT connects resistance with resiliency and focuses on ways in which African American boys and men and systems reject white mainstream cultural hegemony and oppression. AAMT does not completely align with leading resistance or cultural oppositional theorists such John Ogbu and Signithia Fordham (Fordham, 1996; Fordham & Ogbu, 1986; Ogbu, 1991). We are more interested in how the theory has been nuanced by others. For example, Ogbu suggested that some African Americans reject education because it is perceived as supporting their oppression. Bush (1997) challenged Ogbu (1991) by arguing that he has confounded the terms education and schooling. Bush saw schooling as the process used to maintain and continue asymmetrical power relations while he defined education as "the process that should make people more capable of manifesting who they are as defined by their cultural and community norms" (p. 99). Thus, he contended that what Ogbu found in his study was a rejection of schooling by African Americans rather than education as African Americans have always thirsted and fought for education even in the face of tremendous adversity and minimal resources (Anderson, 1988; Bush, 1997; Bush et al., 2006). Solórzano and Bernal (2001) have also reconceptualized Ogbu's theory in a manner that is of interest to AAMT. They asserted that Ogbu focuses on self-defeating resistance while they view some opposition as having transformative qualities, effects, and outcomes as some individuals view society as being unjust and engage in resistant actions as a means of fostering social and political change.

AAMT approaches all forms of resistance and opposition demonstrated by African American boys and men as a strength though some of its manifestations may be counterproductive to what is viewed as being successful or productive in white mainstream society. Moreover, in accordance with tenets of AAMT, we aim to explore how resistant behaviors are connected to or a result of attempts to maintain a continuity and continuation of African culture, consciousness, and biology.

e.   *Race and racism coupled with classism and sexism have a profound impact on every aspect of the lives of African American boys and men.*

Like CRT, AAMT sees racism as an omnipresent force and factor in society. AAMT is particularly interested in how it impacts the lives of African American boys and men. Moreover, AAMT is also interested in understanding how being male and of a certain class may gain some African American boys and men privilege in certain situations (Cannon, 1988; Collins, 1990; hooks, 2000) and more oppression in other spaces (Curry, 2017) and thereby seeks to be in dialogue with such perspectives.

f.  *The focus and purpose of study and programs concerning African American boys and men is for the pursuit of social justice.*

The intent of AAMT is to undermine oppression by explicitly investigating and attending to those practices, policies, programs, systems, concepts, and institutions that promote its continuation (Young, 1990). Yet, AAMT is not a reactionary theory. The aim is not necessarily to respond to cultural hegemony and racism but rather to explicitly account for it, as AAMT works to draw upon the historical and current culture, consciousness, and community to determine what is social justice and freedom for African American boys and men.

## A MOVE AWAY FROM DEFICIT FRAMEWORKS: THE LION, HUNTER, AND SUCCESS

All six tenets of AAMT provide the necessary space and tools to fully examine and perhaps explain the outcomes, behaviors, and experiences of African American boys and men from a free Black thought perspective. Different from other theoretical and conceptual frameworks, AAMT accounts for spiritual matters and provides a directive for what is considered *success*. Both of these concepts, that is, spiritual matters and defining success absent of decolonized thought, are paramount to the following discussion of the fourth tenet of AAMT and for challenging the so-called nondeficit models for which many scholars are calling.

A large cadre of scholars have outright called for an end to negative approaches to researching, theorizing, and writing about African American boys and men and have tended to stigmatize and label the approach as a deficit model. They have done so in such important work as *How Does It Feel to Be a Problem? Black Male Students, Schools, and Learning in Enhancing the Knowledge Base to Disrupt Deficit Frameworks* (Howard, 2013), *(Re)defining the Narrative: High-Achieving Nontraditional Black Male Undergraduates at a Historically Black College and University* (Goings, 2016), and *An Anti-Deficit Achievement Framework for Research on Students of Color in STEM* (Harper, 2010).

This growing call to move from deficit to nondeficit frameworks (Brown, 2011; Brown & Donnor, 2011; Coleman & Davis, 2020; Goings, 2015; Haddix, 2009; Harper, 2010; Howard & Flennaugh, 2011; Stevens, 2021) is being described as a paradigm shift. Howard (2013) provides an understanding of what underlies the call for this shift:

> Therefore, conceptual and theoretical frames that are centered on a discourse of them being endangered, extinct, or at-risk when discussing Black males lend themselves to identifying problems with them, without any institutional or structural critique. This shift calls for researchers to dismiss deficit-laden frames and to move toward a more asset-based approach, which recognizes the strengths, promise, and potential of students and can lead to opening up research approaches that delve into a more comprehensive, nuanced, complex, and authentic account of them. What is essential for social scientists concerned with Black male achievement and experiences in schools to do is to engage in a paradigm shift of how Black males are viewed, studied, and understood. (pp. 62–63)

Essential to this paradigm shift is the notion that African American boys and men need to be in control of their own narratives. Scholars utilize the work of hooks (1990) to underscore this point, as she warns against the precarious predicament of having others, white scholars in particular provide voice to and an analysis of the experiences of African American boys and men. To illuminate this point, Howard (2013) and Goings (2015) draw upon the following two African proverbs, respectively: "Do not let the lion tell the giraffe's story" and "Until the lion tells his side of the story, the tale of the hunt will always glorify the hunter."

We support the move away from deficit-laden frames to frames that enable individuals to tell their own story. We contend, however, that this move is not so much a paradigm shift as a change in position within the same model or prescribed box. The telling of more positive stories is refreshing and necessary, but a paradigm shift requires a different lens by and a box within which to examine and understand both the so-called deficit-laden and nondeficit frames. It is difficult to hear the authentic voice of the lion if he is using the hunter's research methods and frameworks for analysis, definitions, and parameters for success and ontological perspectives about what it is to be a lion. With this in mind, we created the following proverb that we will utilize to portray the distinction between the existing position of the body of literature and the point we are advancing in this present work. Further, the proverb, "Just because the lion is talking doesn't mean that he isn't still telling the hunter's story," will be used to frame the rest of our discussion concerning AAMT and working toward pursuing Sankofic (re)search and free Black thought.

The fourth tenet of AAMT asserts that all forms of resistance and opposition demonstrated by African American boys and men are strengths. Moreover, AAMT calls into question the very notion of resistance and opposition by arguing that a significant amount of what we label as such is a natural or a collective way of being, which white systems and institutions are in opposition to and resist (Bush et al., 2004). To fully explicate these points, we need to dig deeper into oppositional theory and "acting white," using the robust utility of AAMT.

There is a long history of persistent critiques of the hegemonic origin and structure of the *educational* system in the United States. The system is characterized as oppressive (Freire, 1993), deculturizing (Spring, 2016), and miseducating (Woodson, 1990/1933), among a myriad related pejorative assessments (Giroux, 1983a, 1983b; Hill, 1987; McLaren, 2005). Despite these critiques, we have no answer to the question of whether the educational system produces Black people who are essentially white in terms of consciousness and behavior as the body of empirical literature is nonexistent on the matter. Instead, scholars focus on relating the persistent educational and social disparities of African American children, boys in particular, to whether they are perceived as "acting white" for being academically successful (Stinson, 2010). To this end, the dialectical notion that African American students are isolated and mocked systematically by their peers for being academically successful is not clearly established in the literature (Toldson & Owens, 2010).

We have established here that there is a salient difference between education and schooling and that many who are connected to the acting-white discourse have confounded the two. There is no sustained record of humanity rejecting education as we have defined it. Nevertheless, schooling—the process that leaves one oppressed, deculturized, miseducated, and perhaps in the case of African Americans, white, is always contested terrain in one form or another.

W.E.B. Du Bois (2001), in *The Education of Black People: Ten Critiques, 1906–1960*, directly addresses this notion of Black people becoming white as a consequence of such systems as schooling. This perspective is imperative to understanding the broader and deeper view of resistance, ontology, and "acting white" and to theorizing about the outcomes and behaviors of African American boys and men. Du Bois, in a speech to Black teachers in the early 1960s, stated:

> Are we to assume that we will simply adopt the ideals of Americans and become what they are or want to be and that we will have in this process no ideals of our own? That would mean that we would cease to be Negroes as such and become white in action if not completely in color. We would take on the culture of white Americans, doing as they do and thinking as they think. Manifestly this would not be satisfactory. Physically it would mean that we would be integrated with Americans losing first of all, the physical evidence of color and hair and racial type. We would lose our memory of Negro history and of those racial peculiarities which have long been associated with the Negro. (pp. 193–194)

Du Bois' work is profound and informative for our position. Yet, it still does not shed light on the spiritual dynamics of African American boys and men situated in white hegemonic systems, such as schools. This is an issue not often raised in the social science literature, and there are limited theoretical frameworks that encourage scholars to engage such matters, even though, in most empirical studies in which the voice of the participants are central, African American boys and men point to spirituality as a significant factor in their *success* and sustainability (Barnes, 2011; Bonner, 2010; Harmon, 2002; Hunter & Davis, 1992; Watts, 1993). Thus, we turn to the work of Malidoma Somé, a renowned African traditional priest and healer, to assist in the illumination of spiritual matters.

Somé (1994), in his autobiographic work, *Of Water and the Spirit: Ritual, Magic, and Initiation in the Life of an African Shaman*, tells the story of his being kidnapped from a traditional African community in Burkina Faso at the age of 5 by a French Jesuit missionary. He was forced to attend seminary school until he escaped at the age of 20 and returned to live with his family.

He had a challenging time with adjusting to life back among the Dagara people because it was apparent to everyone in his traditional community that the schooling process had inculcated in him a foreign spirit. This is seen in the following quotes, the last of which is a conversation between Malidoma and his father:

> Knowing what you know is not common. It means that you have received the white man's Boar. His spirit lives in you. In a way you are not home yet. It's as if the real you is somewhere else, still trying to find the route home. The you sitting here in front of me is like the priest who came here fifteen years ago and took you away from us. Your soul is in his hands. (p. 176)

> "So why am I of such great concern?"

> "I have already explained that. You carry something in you, something very subtle, something that comes from your contact with the whites—and now you want to be here where you once belong. You cannot live here as you are without turning this place into what you are." (p. 176)

Yet, psychologist Amos Wilson (1999) echoes Somé by positing that African Americans, through harmful spirit possession, become white in spirit and in body:

> What do we mean when we talk about incarnation? We are dealing with the Latin root carnes which has to do with meat, flesh. In other words, the spirit comes to dwell in our very flesh and comes to sculpt our very bodies. Therefore, the spirit is a physical thing as much as it is a psychological thing. The bodies that we have tonight, ladies and gentlemen, are bodies that have been created by the European experience and are not our natural bodies as Afrikan people. Just as the surface of our bodies reflects the influence of another people, the very internal nature and the physiology of our bodies reflect those people as well. (p. 102)

Although scholars may debate the notion that the European schooling process infuses a white spirit into Black people, recall from Chapter 1 that much of the world, from antiquity to present, understands that the educational process is a spiritual and sacred endeavor. We view schooling and education as having the same obligations, functions, and consequences as church, religion, ritual, and other spiritual practices. In other words, church and school are one and the same. Nevertheless, an emerging group of scholars also see schooling from a spiritual perspective as they frame what is happening as a result of schooling as spirit murdering (Love, 2016). Beyond systems of schooling, harmful spirit possession is possible anywhere under the system of white supremacy (Welsing, 1974), but it becomes less probable in isolated settings, such as the inner city or in the segregated south, where Black people in large numbers still live communally, in multigenerational settings and practice "old-time religion," whereby individuals are more likely to get possessed by the Holy Ghost, speak Ebonics, and grow and cook their own food. Thus, harmful spirit possession becomes more probable in integrated situations where African Americans are less likely to do any of the aforementioned. Further, some of the literature on "acting white" found that African American students were far more likely to be seen in that manner in settings in which they were significantly the numerical minority (Austen-Smith & Fryer, 2005).

If schooling is a harmful spirit-possession mechanism, then what we are witnessing in classrooms, institutions, and society in general is a battle of spirits. It is the AAMT's subsystem level, which encompasses matters of the supernatural and spirit, collective will, collective unconscious, and archetypes, that provides fuel for and insight into all forms of resistance and opposition demonstrated by African American boys and men as strengths as well as the basis for examining and understanding both the so-called deficit-laden and nondeficit frames.

Black boys, particularly in inner cities or ghettos, which offer a type of protection against harmful spirit possession, attempt to fight to continue to be African in their spirits. In short, Black boys are expressing: "I don't want your white spirit in me, and I will do whatever it takes to maintain myself to continue to be … a lion." This phenomenon manifests in behaviors such as sagging pants or hats turned backward, braided or locked hair, over-the-teeth grills (gold/silver), and tattoos. In addition, the attempt to maintain an African identity and spirit can be seen in common names and nicknames, such as Davonte, DeAndre, Deante, DeOntario, Cavasia, Tay, Kareem, Jamal, Shaquille, and Mookie. Many of us make fun of these above names and actions; yet, the structure of the language used follows West African linguistic rules and patterns (Smith & Crozier, 1998). Note that it is not our belief that these behaviors occur in reaction to or in opposition to being in colonial institutions, as the lion does not roar because of the hunter; it roars because it is a lion. Wilson (1999) has argued that some inner-city youth participate in Black-on-Black violence or use the N-word, for example, because they are possessed with an alien (white) spirit. Yet, he also has argued that these behaviors occur due to a lack of an African historical narrative that causes cultural amnesia or being *(dis)membered* (Wilson, 1993, 2011).

We are not opposed to the former argument, as the two concepts are not necessarily mutually exclusive, but we favor the latter. Hood or hip-hop culture is not an attempt at or a manifestation of whiteness or harmful spirit possession any more than the lion's roar, which is a manifestation of or an attempt to be a hunter or of being possessed with the hunter's spirit. Rather, these behaviors represent the cultural continuity of Africa in the Americas (Fortes, 1967; Herskovits, 1959; Kenyatta, 1983; McAdoo, 1988; Nobles, 1980; Sudarkasa, 1980), albeit through a clouded lens and the lack of an intact cultural memory or historical narrative. This phenomenon is equivalent to what happens to a white light that passes through an object or filter, becoming distorted, bent, or even taking on colors.

Let us have you return to your pre-Chapter 2 exercises concerning how you position Black boys and men, defining success, the lion and the hunter, and learning to recognize and develop free Black thought. When the authors of this current text imagine a lion in a classroom, we see him being completely disruptive to the schooling process and setting, knocking over tables and chairs, not listening to any commands, directives, lessons, or instructions from the hunter–teacher. There are only two plausible outcomes that we consider as success for the lion: He is either going to eat the hunter–teacher on his way out the door and return to his natural habitat or the hunter–teacher drugs, jails, or kills him. Indeed, if lions were telling their own story, volumes would be written about successful lions who maintained their identity, kept their manes, names, and roar, who dropped out of school, and perhaps even those who were jailed. Lions would enshrine these successful lions in poems and songs, particularly those who remained most unlike the hunter–teacher in any possible way. Free-thinking lion (re)searchers (i.e., free lion thought) would overwhelmingly focus on how these lions were successful under these adverse conditions and somewhat spend time theorizing about unsuccessful lions who *matriculated* and *persisted* through schools and received a diploma in *hunterology*.

Now let us apply our story of the lion and the hunter to how we currently theorize about Black boys and men. Though we did not ask you the following directly, the implied question in the pre-chapter exercise was as follows: Which group of men, the men in prison or the men in college, would you define as successful? Can you imagine theorizing that Black boys and men in prison are more successful than those in college? Only free Black thought can lead you to a space for this theorized position. Remember our new adage: *Just because the lion is talking doesn't mean that he isn't still telling the hunter's story.* With this in mind, add to this adage that caged lions often tell the hunter's story. The overwhelming body of research on Black boys and men is conducted by Black men and can be described as plantation scholarship in that we use colonial tools, frames, and research methodologies to continue to describe and reify life on the plantation, or put another way, we are stuck on a continuous loop for finding more creative ways and terminology of retailing our *dismemberment*. Moreover, almost all the research, irrespective of the race of the researcher, examines or studies Black boys and men under the most confined and narrow possibilities and parameters. Can you imagine a Zoologist interested in understanding the natural behaviors of lions ONLY STUDYING LIONS IN A CAGE! Yet, plantation and caged studies are the two best descriptors of the current state of scholarship on Black boys and men.

The direct question we asked in the exercise was which Black man is more successful: Davonte, who dropped out of school because, among other things, he could never sit still in class, "sags," code switches between slang and Ebonics, and is in and out of jail, or William, who speaks "perfect" English, is clean-cut, and has several degrees and a well-paying job at a Fortune 500 company? What is important in trying to address this question is that, as scholars, we really do not have theories and frameworks by which to position Davonte as being successful. Society, in general, including scholars, is conditioned to see him as deficient, to perhaps to be ashamed of his language, name, and clothing. In fact, Davonte is advised that, to be successful, he needs to distance himself from a ghettoized way of being and his own community and neighborhood, as to get out of the hood or ghetto is seen as the only pathway to success (Bush et al., 2020). Likewise, as scholars, we do not have the theoretical foundations to render William unsuccessful. Rather, scholars write plenty about how he is successful.

A Sankofa (Re)search Model, rooted in AAMT and free Black thought, creates the pathway for scholars to *go back, again and again,* to (re)member and (re)store Devonte's disdained and (dis) membered body. Using this (re)search approach, we can reposition, reintroduce, and (re)birth Devonte in a way that would have a lasting and transformative impact on how we think about, engage, and research Black boys and men, and perhaps how we, as Black men, see ourselves. This, in turn, holds liberating and healing power for both the researched and the researcher.

## REFLECTION QUESTIONS

- What concepts in Chapter 2 were the most challenging for you, and which resonated with you the most?
- If you fully embraced AAMT, how would this impact your practice and research approach?

# CHAPTER 3

## An Ontological and Methodological Mismatch

Utilized by various fields and disciplines, qualitative and quantitative research inquiries are the most commonly employed research methodologies that are hallmarks of the positivist, interpretive, and critical research models or paradigms. We will explore these classic paradigms by outlining their ontological, epistemological, axiological, and methodological components. As you read these perspectives, be particularly attentive to their ontological positions as we would argue that all engagement by human beings, including you, the researcher, is inextricably dependent on what one understands or holds as the nature of being. As you read, ask yourself what it means to be human, what is the person, and which paradigm best explains you and your nature as a human being. Moreover, consider how the answers to these questions influence your thoughts regarding the capacity of these paradigms and methodologies to capture, explain, and predict you and your ability to know and the process of knowing.

# POSITIVIST RESEARCH PARADIGM

According to Park et al. (2020), the positivist research model is strongly aligned with and rooted in quantitative inquiry. The Enlightenment period, where quantitative and positivist perspectives appear to merge, marked a departure from medieval notions of truth. Inspired by scientific advancements, thinkers of this era advocated for an approach to understanding the world grounded in observation, measurement, and the rigorous application of the scientific method (Adams et al., 2005; Uzun, 2016).

According to McDougal (2017), quantitative research appears to be the natural apparatus for the positivist model. It is concerned with and committed to objectivity and measurement to produce replicable outcomes using controlled experimentation by controlling variables. Utilizing hypothesis testing, quantitative researchers collect and utilize data in the form of numbers to determine, by statistical analysis, cause-and-effect relationships, correlations, and patterns. In doing so, quantitative research aligns with the broader positivist philosophy by striving to produce knowledge independent of subjective interpretations and applicable across various contexts (Killam, 2013; Nuryatno, 2003).

Below are the basic constructs of quantitative research. We cover the ontological, epistemological, axiological, and methodological components as they are situated in a positivist model.

## Ontology

Objectivity is the cornerstone of the positivist ontological position, which is connected to the notion of neutrality. Objectivity requires researchers to minimize or eliminate biases, emotions, and opinions to maintain a neutral stance in researching an external reality. In this light, pursuing measurability is a crucial aspect of this paradigm, emphasizing quantifiable data to enable statistical analysis and the identification of patterns. Positivist ontology supports the notion of universal generalizations, seeking to derive laws and principles applicable across different contexts (Aliyu et al., 2014). From this ontological view, phenomena and the person are viewed as being observable and measurable and can be studied using scientific and objective measurements and methods. The person or subject is seen as passive, and thus, positivism supposes that reality exists independently of individual perceptions (Junjie & Yingxin, 2022). Moreover, the person is viewed as a product of their environment and social structures, and external factors shape their behavior. In general, this perspective is less attentive to the role of subjective experience, emotions, and personal agency in shaping human behavior (Aliyu, 2014; Creswell, 2009; Guba & Lincoln, 1994; Killam, 2013; Uzun, 2016).

## Epistemology

From a positivist epistemological perspective, reality is largely material, and knowledge is acquired from an objective scientific method (Guba & Lincoln, 1994; Ikram & Kenayathulla, 2022; Nuryatno, 2003). This knowledge can be best understood by using numbers from statistical analysis. The research process must be controlled to produce replicable and valid results. The researched and the researcher are not connected, and this distance must be maintained to ensure objectivity, that is, to produce uncontaminated research.

## Axiology

Explicit to the positivist research paradigm is that it values value-free research. According to Park et al. (2020), the rejection of subjectivity highlights the importance of preserving an objective position and research practice. In fact, the more distant the researcher is in all aspects of the research process, the better (Aliyu et al., 2014). This presumed distance is even demonstrated in how scholars referred to themselves as "the author" or "the researcher" instead of first-person pronouns such as "I" or "we."

## Methodology

Quantitative research employs various methods to systematically collect and analyze numerical data, facilitating the exploration of patterns, relationships, and statistical significance. Surveys and questionnaires are standard instruments, allowing researchers to gather standardized responses from a large sample (Ikram & Kenayathulla, 2022; McDougal, 2017). Larger sample sizes are favored, aiming for generalizable tendencies, causes, and a presumed more accurate understanding of reality (Al-Ababneh, 2020; Guba & Lincoln, 1994; McDougal, 2017). These methods are guided by a positivist notion of controlled experimentation and a deductive scientific process where variables can be controlled and manipulated (Aliyu et al., 2014; Park et al., 2020).

The testing of theories and hypotheses is central to the quantitative approach, whether utilizing descriptive statistics to apply statistical analysis to calculate averages and percentages or applying other statistical methods, such as correlational research, to analyze the relationships between two or more variables. Observational techniques are also used to collect numerical data about phenomena or behavior, and regression analysis to find the relationship between variables to predict outcomes (Guba & Lincoln, 1994; McDougal, 2017).

## Rigor

Rigor in quantitative research refers to the stringent adherence to scientific practices that eliminate bias to maintain an objective position (Guba & Lincoln, 1994). This is achieved by employing clear and straightforward research questions, appropriate sample sizes (Junjie & Yingxin, 2022; Park et al., 2020), random sampling, standard data collection instruments, and statistical analysis. These measures are taken to produce results that are valid in that the study measures what it intended to measure and is reliable in its ability to produce similar results under similar conditions (McDougal, 2017).

# INTERPRETIVE RESEARCH PARADIGM

Seemingly paradoxical to the positivist paradigm where objectivity is central, the interpretive model foundation rests on subjectivity or at least the notion that it is almost impossible to escape a subjective reality. Subjectivity, in the interpretive approach, represents the idea that a researcher's biases, personal beliefs, experiences, and background influence every aspect of the research process, from the choice of topic, the types of research questions asked, and certainly the interpretation of data and results. To this end, the interpretive research model focuses on the subjective meanings that individuals subscribe to their lives or their lived experiences to interpret events, experiences, behavior, and other social phenomena. Using inductive reasoning, qualitative approaches under the interpretive paradigm work more from the space of building theory rather than testing a hypothesis or a preexisting theory while considering the social, political, historical, and cultural context in which phenomena occur to grasp a more accurate or fuller, and perhaps deeper meaning (Merriam, 1998; Merriam & Tisdell, 2015; Savin-Baden & Major, 2023).

## Ontology

The ontological stance of the interpretive paradigm acknowledges the existence of multiple subjective realities, and the person is the phenomenon that authors the understanding of subjective reality through experiences, narratives, and interpretations. Unlike the positivist's perspective that assumes a single, objective reality, interpretivists recognize that individuals and groups construct their own meanings and interpretations of the world (Merriam, 1998; Merriam & Tisdell, 2015; Nuryatno, 2003). Rooted in the wheelhouse of the ontology of the interpretive paradigm, the notion of multiple realities, allows for a deeper understanding of diverse and nuanced phenomena (Ikram & Kenayathulla, 2022; Junjie & Yingxin, 2022).

Epistemology

How the person comes to know arrives out of one's subjective reality and experiences, which are continually evolving. Thus, knowledge is acquired through continued interpretation and engagement (Ikram & Kenayathulla, 2022; Merriam, 1998; Merriam & Tisdell, 2015; Nuryatno, 2003), which under an interpretive paradigm, positions that knowledge is fluid and dynamic. From this perspective, there is no singular truth. Instead, knowledge and truth are contextual (Nuryatno, 2003).

Axiology

Interpretive research values the subjective meanings the person attributes to their experiences rather than seeking an objective truth (Aliyu et al., 2014). Thus, a person's lived experience is highly valued and is primary in constructing knowledge and understanding behaviors and phenomena. The researcher is not positioned as a detached entity from the research process; instead, the researcher is valued and seen as a co-constructor of meaning and knowledge (Ikram & Kenayathulla, 2022).

*Methodology*

The interpretive paradigm is associated with a qualitative research approach. This model focuses on the subjective experiences and meaning individuals apply to their lives within a social and cultural context (Al-Ababneh, 2020; Guba & Lincoln, 1994; Ikram & Kenayathulla, 2022; Merriam, 1998; Merriam & Tisdell, 2015). It relies on qualitative data collection methods to foster an in-depth, rich, and nuanced understanding of behaviors, events, and other phenomena. Qualitative data are analyzed to find themes and patterns with the aim more toward understanding the *why* of human behavior and social phenomena rather than *how many*, which is the case under the positivist quantitative paradigm (Merriam, 1998; Merriam & Tisdell, 2015). The interpretive paradigm, in comparison with the objective and distant approach explicit in the positive model, puts the researcher in closer proximity to the researched in terms of how data are collected, analyzed, and applied in the production of results and knowledge. Data are collected primarily through in-depth interviews that allow for a back-and-forth dialogue; participant observations close the proximity to the researched, and focus groups create a dynamic space for meaning to come forth (Merriam, 1998; Merriam & Tisdell, 2015; Savin-Baden & Major, 2023).

## Trustworthiness

In qualitative research, trustworthiness is assessed by the degree to which a study's findings are credible, transferable, dependable, and confirmable (Al-Ababneh, 2020; Merriam, 1998; Merriam & Tisdell, 2015). Credibility is the extent to which a study's data reflect participants' experiences; transferability, sometimes called generalizability, is concerned with whether the results of a study can be applied to other situations and populations; dependability or reliability refers to the extent to which a study can produce the same results using the same approach and methods; and, confirmability is the ability to ascertaining that a study's findings are not due to a researcher's bias. Trustworthiness is established by qualitative research methods such as using multiple collecting data methods to support a particular theme or phenomenon, which is called triangulation, providing thick descriptions of narratives to support claims, member checking and peer debriefing, which involves sharing the data and results with the study's participants or other colleagues, and reflecting on the research process by the researcher to see where biases may influence the work (Al-Ababneh, 2020).

# CRITICAL RESEARCH

A critical research approach, grounded in critical theory, is chiefly concerned with asymmetrical power relations. The purpose of research is to uncover such cultural chauvinism and social inequalities. It aims to disrupt the status quo and mainstream narratives by criticizing the reproduction of knowledge, mainly who produces it and who benefits from it. Facilitating social change is at the center of this research approach.

## Ontology

Similarly to the interpretive paradigm, the critical research model positions reality as nonobjective or unfixed (Scotland, 2012). However, it distinguishes itself from other paradigms in that it centers on the notion that power relations and dynamics, and social status profoundly shape knowledge, knowing, and reality (Guba & Lincoln, 1994; Killam, 2013; Nuryatno, 2003; Scotland, 2012). It looks at and beyond the person, as the person is entrapped in a host of power dynamics, and at larger political and social issues to interpret and construct meaning (Killam, 2013; Nuryatno, 2003).

## Epistemology

Knowledge, and therefore reality, is deeply influenced and shaped by power, which is politically and socially constructed. Research and researchers are immensely embedded in this politically constructed view of reality and, therefore, are always non-neutral participants. Objectivity is a rudimentary fallacy. Critical researchers often emphasize the importance of hearing marginalized voices and perspectives that may be excluded in more traditional research paradigms to disrupt mainstream narratives and expand who can produce knowledge (Guba & Lincoln, 1994; Killam, 2013; Nuryatno, 2003; Uzun, 2016; Scotland, 2012).

## Axiology

The critical research paradigm is explicitly a value-laden approach. In fact, the critical approach positions all research paradigms in this light. From this unneutral perspective, critical research approaches value and embrace research that directly aims to counter existing power relationships. Critical researchers often align their work with equality, equity, and social transformation values (Killam, 2013; Uzun, 2016; Scotland, 2012).

## Methodology

In adherence to its ontological, epistemological, and axiological tenets, a critical research methodology aims to uncover asymmetrical power relations and structures. The researcher silently works from the space that neither they, as the researcher, nor the researched exists in a reality beyond the parameters of power (Guba & Lincoln, 1994). Therefore, the researcher must be acutely aware of their positionality as well as the larger society's position of power and engage in ongoing reflection as these both influence knowledge production (Aliyu et al., 2014; Guba & Lincoln, 1994; Scotland, 2012). To question power arrangements and oppression, a critical research methodology employs critical ethnography to study culture and power, critical discourse analysis, feminist research, and other critical approaches with the same social justice aims.

## Trustworthiness

Trustworthiness in the critical research model is similar to the concepts and methods outlined above in the interpretive paradigms. Critical research also includes triangulation, member checking, thick descriptions, and reflectivity to address bias (Uzun, 2016). However, additional emphasis is placed on reflexivity, which expands into the concept of praxis. The cycle of praxis in critical research not only includes reflection or reflexivity, but it also includes action. Critical researchers employ reflection, critical dialog about power arrangements, action, and additional reflection to move toward social justice and change (Scotland, 2012).

Most texts on research methodologies, after providing an overview of the different research approaches, provide the reader with a discussion of the pros and cons or most common critiques of such models. While these conversations are useful, we will not offer that here as what we strive to get to in our current text is somewhat beyond such discussions. Instead, we want to continue to assert that the researcher and their positionality and ontological perspectives are the most influential aspect of the research process; the research methodology, in this line of thinking, that is, qualitative versus quantitative approaches, matters less. That said, we must spend a moment here to reposition quantitative methods.

As McDougal (2017) contends, there is a fundamental difference in how Afrocentric scholars understand the nature of knowledge, rejecting the positivist notion that all valid knowledge is external. Though the Afrocentric approach essentially views reality as spirit, he asserts that this does not take away from the Afrocentric scholar's responsibility to learn how to quantitatively conduct measurements of their positioning of reality as spirit.

The Sankofa (Re)search Model seeks to separate and reclaim quantitative methods from a positivist paradigm to further build on McDougal's point. Many social scientists and African-centered scholars have *thrown the baby out with the bathwater*, failing to decouple positivist perspectives and quantitative methods. We assert that quantitative reasoning, assessment, measurement, and research represent pure and free Black thought and practice, nature, and spirit. Moreover, it is African people who introduced this scientific methodology (Van Sertima, 1984) to the world in an attempt to understand and quantify the mundane and the supernatural (spirit) aspects of life and the universe.

Let us first look at the mundane use of African quantitative practices in the ancient African world. Though we separated the mundane from the supernatural here for discussion, later in this chapter, we will make the case that they are inextricably linked or even the same.

The Ishango Bone, discovered near the Semliki River in the Democratic Republic of Congo, is a fibula bone with a series of notches carved into its surface. Dating back approximately 20,000 to 25,000 years ago, it is believed to have been used as a mathematical tool or tally stick. The notches on the Ishango Bone are arranged in three columns, with patterns suggesting an understanding of prime numbers, systematic incrementation, and geometric organization. Similarly, the Lebombo Bone, discovered in the Lebombo Mountains between South Africa and Swaziland, shares similarities with the Ishango Bone in its function as a counting tool. Carved with a series of notches along one edge, the Lebombo Bone dates back approximately 35,000 years. While smaller than the Ishango Bone, it appears to have served a similar purpose, possibly as a lunar calendar, a device for tracking the passage of time, or an instrument used and developed by African women to track their menstrual cycles (Bangura, 2011). Like its counterpart, the Lebombo Bone demonstrates the mathematical sophistication of ancient societies, revealing a deep understanding of observation and the collection of quantitative data (research), numerical concepts, assessment, and computation, and the ability to apply them for practical purposes (Bangura, 2011).

Another salient example of the clear usage of quantitative research methods as a mundane and practical application produced by free Black thought was the employment of surveys in the ancient Nile Valley (Barnard, 2001). Pharaohs conducted surveys of farmers to assess agricultural productivity, land usage, and taxation. To conduct these surveys, the pharaohs likely employed a team of scribes, officials, and surveyors who visited villages and settlements to gather information directly from farmers (Paulson, 2005). These surveys provided valuable data that informed decisions, or what we now call data-driven decision-making (Brynjolfsson & McElheran, 2016), regarding land allocation, resource management, and taxation policies.

While undoubtedly there was a practical impetus for the development and function of quantitative methods and ancient mathematics, they were also developed out of an ongoing attempt to explain and quantify the laws of God (Spirit). Amen (2003) writes, from a pure Black thought viewpoint that mathematics "allows us to acquire knowledge of the existence of all quantifiable events that cannot be perceived through the senses" (p. 31). In ancient Nile Valley civilizations, the laws of God were embodied and captured in the Goddess Maat (African Creation Energy, 2010; Amen, 2003; Karenga, 2004). There is considerable disagreement as to whether, from an etymological perspective, the word mathematics is derived from the word Maat; nevertheless, there is little disagreement about mathematics being developed and used in the ancient African world as an attempt to explain or know Maat, that is, the laws and the ways of God (Amen, 2003).

Encompassing and beyond this notion of mathematics, Maat, and the laws of God, free Black thought in the Nile Valley positioned numbers as the Gods (Amen, 2003). The primordial Deities were numbered or said another way: a number represented each Deity. Depending on the epoch and location in the Nile Valley, these Gods had a collective appellation for different groups of divinities: the Ennead, meaning The Nine, and the Ogdoad, reflecting the four pairs of divinities to make the eight (Asante & Mazama, 2009). This way of researching, knowing, understanding the Divine, Spirit, numbers, and laws produced sacred mathematics and geometry, which led to the construction of the pyramids that reside today in modern-day Sudan and Egypt.

To crystallize that quantitative methods originated from pure and free Black thought and practice and should be reclaimed as research practices for those interested in healing Black boys and men, we focus on the Ifá binary divination system. Ifá utilizes quantitative methods as a means of knowing and knowledge production.

In general, African divination encompasses various spiritual practices found across the continent, each deeply rooted in cultural traditions and beliefs. These practices serve as channels for communicating with ancestral spirits, deities, and other supernatural entities to seek guidance, insight, and solutions to life's challenges by accessing knowledge of the past, present, and future. African divination often involves the interpretation of signs, symbols, and patterns manifested through rituals, sacred objects, or natural phenomena. Ifá divination traces its origins thousands of years back to the Yoruba people of the present-day Nigeria, Benin, and Togo.

Central to Ifá divination is the belief in Orunmila, the Orisha of wisdom and divination, who is revered as the custodian of Ifá knowledge. Through Orunmila, practitioners of Ifá seek guidance from the spiritual realm, interpreting the messages conveyed through a divination chain containing eight nuts. The mathematical structure of Ifá divination is rooted in binary arithmetic, a system of numerical representation based on two fundamental states: open and closed (Folorunso et al., 2010; Okewande, 2020). (Note that binary mathematics is fundamental to computer science and digital electronics because it forms the basis for digital representation and computation in modern computing systems.) The divination chain consists of eight nuts, each capable of assuming either an open or closed position, resulting in 256 possible combinations. These combinations form specific patterns known as signatures, which trained researchers or priests interpret. The interpretation of Ifá divination relies on the mathematical patterns encoded within the signatures, combined with cultural knowledge, spiritual intuition, and logical reasoning. Each signature or combination of signatures corresponds to one of the 16 principal Ifá literary corpus, called Odu, each with its unique verses, proverbs, and rituals (Folorunso et al., 2010; Karenga, 1999; Okewande, 2020).

In summary, the Ifá system is a quantitative research methodology used to acquire knowledge of the past, present, and future. While it mainly was our intent to use the four aforementioned examples to get the reader to rethink, reposition, and reclaim quantitative research methods under the umbrella of original and free Black thought and practice, we also wanted to discuss the latter example because the Sankofa (Re)search Model for the healing of Black boys and men includes the usage of divination as a (re)search technique as a means of collecting data, knowledge production, and (re)membering.

Nevertheless, if the authors had to choose a research approach based only on the most common and mainstream research approaches discussed above, we would choose an interpretive perspective employing qualitative inquiry. More specifically, we are particularly drawn to narrative inquiry as a qualitative research methodology.

## NARRATIVE INQUIRY AND STORYTELLING

The potency of storytelling holds immense significance for African and other indigenous peoples, serving as a crucial cultural and historical conduit that transcends generations. Within these communities, oral traditions play a central role in preserving and transmitting knowledge, values, and identity (Gbagbo & Elder,

2019). Through the art of storytelling, ancestral wisdom is imparted, encompassing traditions, folklore, spiritual beliefs, and life lessons. The art and act of storytelling is a spiritual process in and of itself that can convey multidimensional meanings and pass down or unlock esoteric knowledge and spiritual awakening (Oamen, 2008, 2011), much like how many Black preachers use it to teach and stir up the Holy Ghost—an unseen broker of knowledge and power.

These narratives also serve as vital oral history repositories, offering alternative perspectives to written accounts and ensuring that the diverse nuances and aspects of their stories and struggles remain acknowledged. Beyond historical documentation, storytelling reinforces social cohesion, bringing communities together around the fire, baobab tree (see Jeffers-Coly, 2022) or other communal spaces to share experiences and strengthen interpersonal bonds. Many stories within African traditions carry spiritual or moral guidance, shaping ethical behavior, community importance, and interconnectedness (Gbagbo & Elder, 2019; Oamen, 2008, 2011; Van Biljon et al., 2018). Furthermore, storytelling has been a potent tool of resistance against colonization, oppression, and cultural erasure, enabling communities to reclaim or continue narratives, to challenge stereotypes, and to be self-determined. It provides a platform for healing and addressing historical traumas (Brewster, 2022; Kaminer, 2006). Through its adaptability and evolutionary nature, storytelling ensures relevance and resilience, allowing communities to incorporate new experiences and challenges into their narratives. In essence, storytelling is not merely a form of entertainment but a dynamic and integral facet of African cultures, shaping worldviews and empowering communities to navigate the complexities of the past, present, and future.

Narrative research uses the powerful tool of storytelling. This method involves collecting and analyzing personal stories, anecdotes, or narratives to gain profound insights into the intricate aspects of human experiences, perspectives, and social phenomena (Wells, 2011). The primary focus of narrative research is understanding the rich meanings people attribute to their experiences and how they construct and communicate these narratives. It relies on the storytelling process, where individuals express their experiences through various mediums such as interviews, written accounts, or life histories (Barkhuizen & Consoli, 2021; Sonday et al., 2020; Wells, 2011). Narrative research emphasizes the importance of contextual understanding, acknowledging the influence of cultural, social, historical, and personal factors shaping an individual's narrative. Researchers engage in the interpretation and analysis of narratives to identify underlying themes, patterns, and meanings (Kim, 2011; Wells, 2012). This approach recognizes the subjective nature of human experiences and adopts a holistic view, considering the interconnectedness of different elements within a story and its broader contextual framework (Pino Gavidia & Adu, 2022). With an emphasis on language and communication, narrative research provides a valuable qualitative method for exploring diverse topics, including identity, culture, learning processes, and social interactions across fields (Kim, 2011).

## (RE)SEARCH LESSONS FROM GEORGE WASHINGTON CARVER

Now that we have provided you with a foundation for the most utilized research approaches, let us return to the questions and reflections posed at the beginning of this chapter. Which paradigm best explains you and your nature as a human being? What are your thoughts regarding the capacity of these paradigms and methodologies to capture, explain, and predict your ability to know and the process of knowing? Do these paradigms and methodologies match or come up short with your perspectives? And how? While you contemplate these matters, we offer the story below about Dr. George Washington Carver. Perhaps you can ascertain by now that we utilize stories as a pedagogical strategy to, among other things, expand notions and constructs of what is possible as it allows us to tap into ancestral wisdom, spiritual beliefs, and life lessons.

This is a good place for a reminder; in Chapter 1, we conveyed to you that under the Sankofa (Healer) (re)search approach, to (re)search is to be relentless and indefatigable, to go back and search again and again for the truth. This kind of pursuit or search may push the researcher beyond the boundaries of Westernized training and quantitative and qualitative empirical measurement tools because studying Black boys and men is a complex, multifaceted, multidimensional, and cosmic and in motion phenomenon. Moreover, in Chapter 2 we introduced the subsystem as part of AAMT. The subsystem offers a space to contemplate various influences and factors, including the super-natural and spirit, the collective will, collective unconscious, and archetypes. It also presents an opportunity to explore multidi-mensional levels of reality as described by physicists, both at the individual level within the microsystem and as an underlying aspect of other systems in the model. In addition, the subsystem represents unknown or unexplained aspects. As Singh (2003) reminds us, there is much yet to be known and studied, particu-larly regarding the significant proportion of the universe composed of unmanifested dark matter or dark energy.

*George Washington Carver's legacy transcends the boundaries of art and science. His words, "Anything will give up its secrets if you love it enough," reflect a profound understanding of the interconnectedness of all living things. Through his love for plants, peanuts, and people, George Washington Carver not only unlocked the secrets of nature but also left an indelible mark on the fields of art, agriculture, and chemistry.*

*As an infant, George Washington Carver faced a turbulent start to life during the closing days of the Civil War. He was born into slavery after Moses and Susan Carver bought his mother, Mary, age 13, from his neighbor. Mary would go on to have several children, including George Washington Carver. After being kidnapped along with his sister and mother by raiders, they were transported to Kentucky and sold. In an effort to recover those who were considered his property, Moses Carver enlisted a bounty hunter. While successful in recovering or re-kidnapping the already previously kidnapped baby George, the bounty hunter couldn't locate the rest of the family. After chattel slavery ended in 1865, Moses and Susan Carver raised him and his brother.*

*As a young boy, Dr. Carver asked Moses Carver about grapes, asking, "Why are grapes purple?" Moses, uncertain about the answer, replied, "Nobody knows." Undeterred, George posed the question to a higher authority, asking, "Does God know?" Moses assured him, saying, "Of course He does." George confidently responded, "Then I'll ask Him," and left the room. Dr. Carver made this a practice at an early age, conversing with God about his purpose in life and various other matters. Moses Carver remarked that he sounded as if he were going to meet God out there, somewhere around the house.*

*At about the age of 12, he left the Carver farm to attend school for the first time and stayed with a couple who took him in exchange for chores. Mrs. Maria Watkins, a midwife who practiced traditional herbal medicine, sparked Dr. Carver's early interest and practice in botany. He quickly became so adept that he became a local authority on diseases and fertilizers, drawing farmers seeking advice for maintaining robust gardens, crops, and orchards. This earned him the nickname "Plant Doctor" for his innate ability to care for and nurture the plants that surrounded him. It was also during this time his fascination with art took root. In fact, regarding the latter, he would start college as an art student before switching to agriculture, going on to paint numerous pictures much later in life.*

*Dr. Carver's conversations with God continued throughout his life, guiding his pursuit of knowledge. His thirst for education led him to Iowa State Agricultural College, where he excelled in botany, eventually becoming the university's first Black faculty member. However, his journey took a turn when Booker T. Washington invited him to join the Tuskegee Institute in Alabama.*

*At Tuskegee, faced with the agricultural and economic crisis of the South, Dr. Carver turned to prayer and nature for information. Rising at 4 or 5 a.m. each day in the solitude of nature, Dr. Carver had conversations with God, trees, plants, and rocks. In a dialogue with God, Dr. Carter asked, "Why did you make the peanut?" To this, God replied with a scientific plan: "Separate it into water, fats, oils, gums, resins, sugars, starches, and amino acids. Then recombine these under My three laws of compatibility, temperature, and pressure. Then you will know why I made the peanut."*

*The renowned scientist Dr. George Washington Carver followed God's directions. A remarkable short time later, over 300 uses for the peanut emerged, ranging from food products like peanut lemon punch to industrial applications such as plastics and cosmetics. His work did not stop at peanuts; he also delved into sweet potatoes, discovering over 100 uses.*

*Considered one of the greatest scientists by many, Dr. Carver's impact reached far beyond the laboratory. His scientific and practical agricultural advice, including crop rotation and diversification, breathed new life into the Southern economy and changed farming worldwide. The once-struggling agricultural region flourished with peanuts and sweet potatoes, ending cotton dependence. When faced with skepticism, he testified before the House Ways and Means Committee for an astounding hour and 45 minutes, captivating them with tales of peanut-based products and his scientific knowledge.*

*In reflecting on his scientific discoveries and knowledge, Dr. Carver profoundly stated, "My discoveries come like a direct revelation from God." Furthermore, he emphasized the intricate connection between nature and divine communication, expressing, "To think of Nature as wireless telegraph stations through*

*which God speaks to us every day, every hour, and every moment*
*of our lives." These sentiments encapsulate his deep reverence for*
*the natural world and a particular methodology for acquiring*
*and advancing scientific knowledge and practice.* (Hersey, 2007;
Kremer, 2017; Mackintosh, 1976; McMurry & Edwards, 1981)

Pause here to address similar questions of the Dr. Carver narrative that we have been posing throughout this chapter. What
do you garner to be the nature of being in the story? Which of
the common research paradigms best explains or aligns with this
definition of being? What was the process of knowing? What is
the capacity of the commonly used paradigms and methodologies to engage in the same process of knowing?

The above narrative is rich with information that challenges the
most common research paradigms and methodologies previously
outlined. It positions what is viewed as unseen and unheard phenomena, and perhaps for many, positioned outside of reality
altogether—that is, God, Spirit, and Nature—as participants in a
researcher's data-gathering process. Moreover, it employs the use
of ritual and love as a research method, tool, or instrument to
acquire knowledge. In fact, ritual and love increase a scientist's
ability to see and hear beyond the parameters set by positivist,
interpretive, and critical paradigms. This begs the question, who
is the researcher, or in other words, who is the person?

## SEEING/HEARING, RITUAL, AND LOVE
## AS (RE)SEARCH METHODS

In the rest of the chapter, we aim to not only address the latter
question concerning personhood, but we will also discuss the
concept of seeing/hearing, ritual, and love as they relate to the
research process in hopes of deepening our ongoing development
of a Sankofa (Re)search Model. Though we will primarily use Dr.
Carver's story as the foundation for our dialogue, it is important

to note that his narrative and methodology for acquiring knowledge are not unique. We have Sojourner Truth, who builds an altar or shrine in the forest, where she, like Dr. Carver, would arise early in the morning to pray, as an ancient African technology for knowing. This ritual and (re)search practice eventually led to an encounter with what she describes as God and the Son of God. Madam C.J. Walker, the great entrepreneur and political and social activist, is recorded to be the first self-made woman millionaire. Her wealth primarily stemmed from hair care products. Her knowledge of the scientific formula for her product came from a (re)search methodology rooted in prayers and dreams. She says that she prayed and one night God answered her prayers through a dream. "In that dream a big Black man appeared to me and told me what to mix up for my hair" (Bundles, 2002, p. 60). Some of the ingredients were grown in Africa. She sent for the items and mixed a concoction. She tried it on herself and some friends, and it proved to be a remedy for growing hair that had been damaged. Even today, we have Bea Dixon, entrepreneur and founder of the company The Honey Pot, which specializes in herbal feminine care products and systems. She employed the same research method as Madam C.J. Walker and others to heal herself and create a company to help others. She writes, "I was suffering with bacterial vaginosis for 8 months when an ancestor came to me in a dream and gifted me with a vision to heal myself. With her help I created The Honey Pot to solve for what other brands wouldn't—feminine care, powered by herbs" (Dixon, 2025).

## Who is the Person?

Again, we argue that the researcher, the person, is the most significant component of the research process irrespective of the employed research paradigm or methodology. One's ontological contentions directly impact one's approach to knowing, ability to know, and the perception of the location of knowledge. This is why from the onset of this current text we provided space for the reader to reflect on who they are and what or who is the nature of the researched particularly in respect of Black boys and men. We hope to deepen our understanding of both the former and the latter with this brief discussion of who is the person.

Nobles (2023) provides us with notable resources to discuss this matter from an African perspective. His discussion of African personhood takes us across time, geography, nations, and cultures in Africa, covering the Kemetic, Zulu, Akan, Yoruba, Bantu, Mende, and Lebou peoples. We will provide a bullet summary of the significant themes of his presentation:

- The person is a living sun who, in human form, knows all that is spirit and has a relationship with the total perceptible and ponderable universe.
- The person is spirit.
- If reality is, seen or unseen, it is spirit.
- The person is human.
- The person is a spirit and a body.
- The person is a person because of other people.
- There is no separation between matter, spirit, and the person.
- All that exists is a concrete expression of spirit.
- All material objects are spiritual energy, including mountains, plants, trees, animals, bodies of water, and the like.
- Matter and the person exist simultaneously in the past, present, and future.
- The person has a coalition of spiritual forces that possess, guide, and protect the person.

While Noble's effort is comprehensive and more than sufficient in capturing the ontological perspectives of African peoples across time, geography, and nations, we aim to further enrich your understanding by directly exposing you to additional African philosophical writings. We hope that these profound writings will have a direct impact on the reader both intellectually and spiritually. Nevertheless, the Zulu Personal Declaration (refer to Asante & Abarry, 1996, pp. 372–378 for the complete statement) unequivocally addresses the question of what constitutes a person from a pure and free African framework.

*The Zulu Personal Declaration*

I

I am

I am alive

I am conscious and aware

I am unique

I am who I say I am

I am the value *UQOBO* [essence]

I forever evolve inwardly and outwardly in response to the challenge of my nature

I am the face of humanity

The face of humanity is my face

I contemplate myself and see everything in me

I perceive; that which I perceive is form

Form is unchanging value

Value is eternal consciousness

Consciousness is that in which all things have their origin

It does not change; it exists from eternity to eternity

It is an infinite cluster of clusters of itself

It is forever evolving in response to the challenge of its nature

It is ULTIMATE VALUE

It is *UQOBO*

The value metamorphoses into a phenomenon

Each phenomenon is a total of smaller forms

Phenomena form clusters to produce other phenomena

The cosmic order is an indefinite total of forms and phenomena

I am a phenomenon; I am a person

I am *UQOBO*; I am consciousness

The infinity is a unity; it cannot be destroyed

I am a constituent of the unity

I cannot be destroyed

The infinity and I are inseparable

I cannot exist outside of the infinity

For, there is no outside of it.

Everything is inside the infinity

*UQOBO* is the Infinity

It is a Whole

It cannot be other than Whole; without me it cannot be Whole

Nothing can be added to or subtracted from the Whole

The infinity is alive

There is no death within it

There is life and perpetual agmination

That which is alive has purpose

Purpose is destiny

Perpetual evolution is the destiny of *UQOBO*

*UQOBO* evolves in response to the challenge of its nature

The *Law* regulates evolution

It is a constituent of *UQOBO*

It is the will of the Infinity

It is my will; it explains everything, for there are no mysteries

Mystery is the redoubt of the ignorant

Everything, everywhere, evolves according to the *Law*

The *Law* is knowable

I cannot violate the *Law* no matter what I do

I incarnate the *Law*

Everything I do translates into action one section of the *Law* of the other

The processes of the *Law* are irreversible

Ultimate Absurdity is the attempt to invert the *Law*

The inversion of the *Law* is a cosmic cataclysm

It is Ultimate Criminality

I am the reconciler of all contradictions

*UQOBO*, the *Law* and I are together the Definite Agminate

Nothing can separate us

I live now

And shall live forever in *UQOBO*

For, I am *UQOBO*

I am eternal; I am the secret that drives out all fear

Perpetual evolution is my destiny

I evolve forever, in response to the challenge of being human

I have a mind to light my path in the mazes of the cosmic order

The mind has many sides

It comprehends all things

It establishes my right to latitude; to be heard

It makes me feel at home in the cosmic order

My neighbour has a mind

It, also, comprehend all things

My neighbour and I have the same origins

We have the same life-experiences and a common destiny

We are the obverse and reverse sides of one entity

We are unchanging equals

We are faces which see themselves in each other

We are mutually fulfilling complements

We are simultaneously legitimate values

My neighbour's sorrow is my sorrow

His joy is my joy

He and I are mutually fulfilled when we stand by each other in moments of need

His survival is a precondition of my survival

That which is freely asked or freely given is love

Imposed love is a crime against humanity

I am sovereign of my life

My neighbour is sovereign of his life

Society is a collective sovereignty

It exists to ensure that my neighbour and I realise the promise of being human

I have no right to anything I deny my neighbour

I am all; all are me

I come from eternity

The present is a moment in eternity

I belong to the future

I can commit no greater crime than to frustrate life's purpose for my neighbour

Consensus is our guarantee of survival

I define myself in what I do to my neighbour.

No community has any right to prescribe the destiny for other communities

This universe I challenge a higher being than me to show

My knees do not quake when I contemplate my destiny

I know my way to eternity

I make obeisances to the million sides of the ciliate mind

The Eternal Person is Universal Man, Universal Woman and Universal Child

I am a Universal Constant; I am a Cosmic Constant

I am All-in-one; I am One-in-All

I am the circle which encompasses infinity

I am the point that is the beginning of the circle

I am *umuntu*, the knower of all probabilities and possibilities

There is nothing I cannot know

There is no tyranny I cannot crush

The value of water is $H_2O$; it lives from eternity to eternity

Nothing exists anywhere which can destroy it

I am who I am

I am not a creature; nothing can destroy me

I am the self-evolving value NTU; I live forever and ever

I am the phenomenon MUNTU (life-force)

I am a person

The African ontological paradigm presents the person, a living sun, as a dynamic entity deeply intertwined with the spiritual and physical realms as the "knower of all probabilities and possibilities." All physical entities, including mountains, plants, trees, animals, bodies of water, and similar phenomena, contain spiritual energy, which is knowable to the individual who embodies or is spirit. From this African ontological perspective presented by Nobles and the Zulu Personal Declaration, Dr. Carver's research approach is represented in his statement, "*To think of Nature as wireless telegraph stations through which God speaks to us every day, every hour, and every moment of our lives*" falls seamlessly into place with free and pure Black thought and ontological perspectives on African personhood.

As a researcher, what if you operated from the ontological perspective we are advancing here, understanding yourself, nature, and Black boys and men from the African paradigm of personhood? How would this influence your methodological approaches such as your means of collecting data in general, but more specifically, data outside of your capacity to hear/see beyond your own eyes and ears? Much of what we are unfolding is contingent on the researcher's ability to see/hear. Think of your training or initiation process as a researcher. What was your training preparing you to do? What were its goals and aims? What was the underlining paradigm, that is, positivist, interpretive, critical or other, of your schooling process to become a researcher? Whatever the approach, did it prepare you to see/hear beyond your physical ears and eyes like Dr. Carver? If not, what training would you need? Compare the goals of your training process to those of the Dagara people of West Africa in the example below.

> Traditional education consists of three parts: enlargement of one's ability to see, destabilization of the body's habit of being bound to one plane of being, and the ability to travel transdimensionally and return. Enlarging one's vision and abilities has nothing supernatural about it; rather, it is natural to be part of nature and to participate in a wider understanding of reality.

> Overcoming the fixity of the body is the hardest part of initiation. As with the seeing exercise, there is a lot of unconscious resistance taking place. There is also a great deal of fear to be overcome. One must travel to the other side of fear, crossing the great plains of terror and panic to arrive at the quiet one feels in the absence of fear. Only then does true transformation really begin to happen. … This metamorphosis cannot happen as long as the body is weighed down by heaviness. One must go through a process of relearning, enforcement of these lessons, and the consolidation of new knowledge. This kind of education is nothing less than a return to one's true self, that is, to the divine within us. (Somé, 1994, p. 226)

How do they compare? We are going to guess that for an overwhelming majority of you, your experience in the training or schooling process greatly mismatches with what is utilized by the Dagara people. Yet, we hope that it is apparent from reading the above excerpt that the Dagara educational process is rooted in and aligns with the African notion of personhood. Similarly, a research methodology anchored in African ontology, in which seeing/hearing from what appears to be invisible entities, should seamlessly match. In the book *The Spirit of Intimacy: Ancient African Teachings in the Ways of Relationships*, Sobonfu Somé (2002) describes a hearing ceremony used for knowing the purpose of an unborn child. The account is an example of a research method that reflects the ontological frames of African peoples.

> When a woman is pregnant, a hearing ritual is performed. In this ritual, elders will ask the unborn child, "Who are you? Why are you coming here? Why do you bother, this world is too messed up what can we do to ease your journey?"
>
> The baby takes over the mother's voice and speaks back, "This is who I am. I am coming to help uphold the knowledge of the ancestors," or, "I am coming to do this or that." And based on that information, the elders will prepare an appropriate ritual space in which to receive the child and make sure that everything is ready here before the child is born.
>
> After the birth, their elders make sure they surround the child with things that will help her remember and accomplish the purpose she has described. And when she reaches adolescence and goes through initiation, she has to go back to the time before she was born to *remember* (emphasis ours) what she said. This is because growing up is a process of forgetting; this body, as the elders say, takes away certain things from us as we grow. Up until the age of five or six, children remember things perfectly, but after that something starts to happen in the body that makes them forget.
>
> At the beginning of the hearing ritual the baby might choose a stone and gives a description of what the stone will look like. The elders will go out and locate the stone by the way it moves or behaves. And that stone, basically, contains all the information about the person. It is through this stone, sitting back in the medicine room in my village, that the elders can monitor what's happening with me here right now. (pp. 56–57)

The above passage is saturated with multiple examples of an African ontological paradigm in practice, which is connected to a research methodological technique of seeing/hearing used to gather data and knowledge. A salient example is the use of nature, in this case a rock (Dr. Carver also spoke of being in dialogue with rocks), as a participant and conduit in the research process. It is important to note that the mechanism or method employed was ritual. The application of ritual situated the person (or researcher) in the position to hear/see. This is evident in the ritual of initiation that removed fear to facilitate seeing/hearing in the excerpt on the Dagara traditional educational system, in the hearing ritual that was used as the procedure enacted to hear the unborn child in the above quote, and in the ritual employed by Dr. Carver of arising at a particular time of day to hear from God and Nature.

## Ritual

Thus, what is ritual? A ritual is a ceremony, practice, or routine with the obligation to call in Spirit to guide, direct, speak, listen, or possess. The components and process of ritual allow the person to connect with other persons, Spirit, and Nature by removing barriers and blocks such as fears that stand between us and Spirit (Somé, 2002). Drumming, movement, songs, prayers, baths, breath, and medicines (herbs) are a few of the instruments and elements used in rituals to create the vibrational alignment with matter, nature, and spirits to allow the individual to see/hear.

Dr. Carver utilized an ancient African (re)search or knowing method in the form of ritual as routine by arising and practicing prayer every day. Moreover, he couples his approach with other ancient ritual data-gathering methods. Gathering data also known as praying in the early morning has long been a research method of African peoples. In some circles, it is called the bewitching hour where some contend that a witch is most powerful. In African spiritual traditions, it is the time when priests pray and conduct spiritual work as it is seen as a time where God and other spirits are most available. Yet, this (re)search method is captured in the Black Christian gospel tradition in the following lyrics:

Late in the midnight hour

God's gonna turn it around

It's gonna work, it's gonna in your favor

Yes it will, yes it will

Late in the midnight hour, yeah

God's gonna turn it around

And around and around and around, yeah

And around and around (Hammond & Radical for Christ, 1995)

Now that we have established ritual as a vital element of the research process for African peoples as an expression of both free Black thought and practice, which is indeed a necessary component of our emerging Sankofa (Re)search Model, it is time to turn our attention to love as another critical factor and research method. Dr. Carver's statement, "Anything will give up its secrets if you love it enough" is ideal for our discussion.

## Love

Sankofa is represented by two Adinkra symbols. We described one in the first chapter as a bird with its head turned backward holding an egg while its feet are facing or moving forward. The other symbol is a stylized heart (see Figure 3.1). In ancient Kemet, the heart held a central and profound significance, far beyond its physiological function.

The heart in Nile Valley civilizations was considered the seat of intelligence, emotions, and memory, making it the most vital organ in defining a person's character and essence. Unlike in some other cultures where the brain was perceived as the locus of intellect, the ancient Africans attributed paramount importance to the heart. The heart was seen as the repository of an individual's true essence, reflecting their moral and ethical qualities.

**Figure 3.1**   Sankofa Heart

Love, which stems from the heart, like ritual, creates a particular vibrational dynamic that increases one's ability to see/hear Spirit for the collection of data. Nobles (2023) underscores this notion of the capacity of love to enlarge hearing/seeing; however, he expands on the construct by also discussing its healing properties:

> ZOLA (love) is magnetic energy with an electrical charge that makes contact and connection between knowing and the knowable Spirits (energy) to cause the activation of Ngolo (healing energy). ZOLA is the energy that causes the activation of molecular/cellular regeneration at both the material and immaterial levels. (pp. 86–97)

Thus, the vibration or energy of love has the capacity to position the person to hear/see matter or phenomena that might normally be undetectable by the physical eyes and ears. This is not a foreign concept in the physical science community and can be explained in a rudimentary manner. For example, humans cannot hear a dog whistle because dog whistles emit ultrasonic frequencies or vibration beyond the range of human hearing. Dog whistles typically produce sounds in the range of 16,000 to 22,000 Hz, while humans can only hear sounds between 20 Hz and 20,000 Hz.

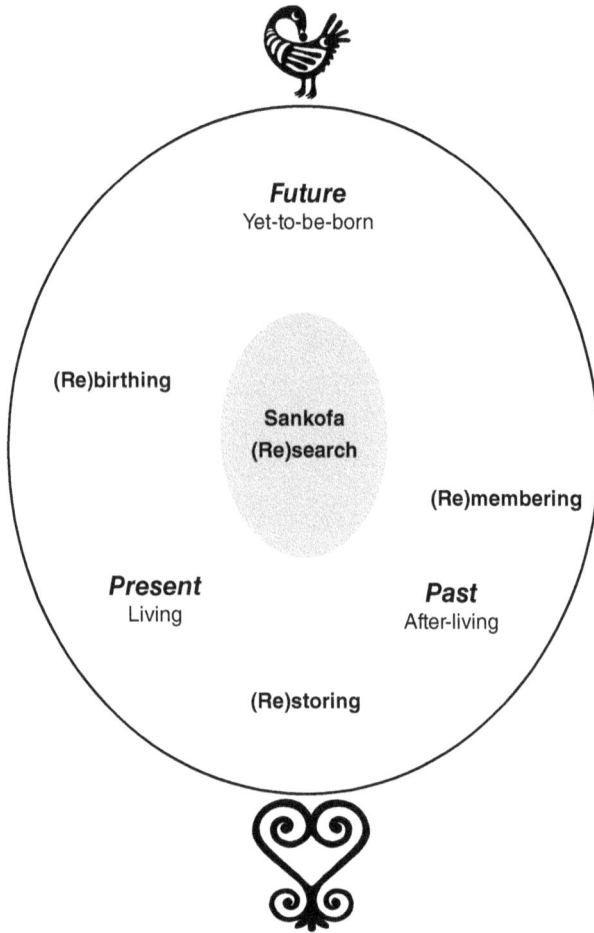

**Figure 3.2**  Sankofa (Re)search Model 2.0

Dogs, however, can hear sounds up to 45,000 Hz, making them sensitive to the high-frequency sounds produced by dog whistles.

Applied to the emerging Sankofa (Re)search Model that situates the (re)searcher as a healer, love is the (re)search method that positions and aligns the researcher to be able to see/hear data from Black boys and men that would otherwise go undetectable or be invisible. In other words, to paraphrase Dr. Carver, *Black boys and men will give up their secrets if you love them enough*. Moreover, love provides the foundation for the possibility for the Sankofic Model to be a healing approach for Black boys and men as it provides, to restate Nobles, "the energy that causes the activation of molecular/cellular regeneration at both the material and immaterial levels." See Figure 3.2 that now depicts that the foundation of the Sankofa (Re)search Model for (re)membering, (re)storing, and (re)birthing Black boys and men is love.

The notion of loving Black boys and men as a research method is entirely paradoxical to a positivist approach, where objectivity is considered the pathway to true knowledge. In social science research, this is related to what is called the etic viewpoint, which is the objective or outsider account (Merriam, 1998). In practice, the more distant the proximity of the researcher to the participants, the more valid or trustworthy the study is perceived to be. The opposite perspective where the researcher is situated in close proximity to the participants is called the subjective, insider, or emic account (Merriam, 1998). It was famed anthropologist and novelist Zorah Neal Hurston who introduced and practiced the latter.

Hurston's approach to research was characterized by her unique blend of creativity, empathy, and deep cultural immersion. Unlike many anthropologists of her time, who approached their subjects with a detached and objective lens, Hurston believed in the importance of establishing personal connections and rapport with the people she studied.

One key aspect of Hurston's approach was her commitment to participant observation, a method commonly used in anthropology. Rather than simply observing from a distance, Hurston actively engaged with the communities she studied, immersing herself in their daily lives, rituals, and traditions.

This hands-on approach allowed her to gain a deeper understanding of their culture and worldview. She saw herself not just as an observer, but as a participant in the communities she studied, valuing their knowledge and perspectives as equal to her own. Another hallmark of Hurston's research was her use of storytelling, which we have already outlined in this chapter as an amicable method to our emerging approach, as a means of documentation. Recognizing the power of narrative to convey cultural values and beliefs, she collected and recorded folk tales, songs, and oral histories from the communities she studied (see Strain, 2023).

To say the least, the Sankofa (Re)search Model is an emic approach enhanced by ritual and love. For an example of a discussion of proximity, Black boys, and men, and trustworthiness, see the excerpt below taken from a qualitative research article studying Black male community college students' study abroad experience in Senegal, West Africa:

> The degree to which one can find our study trustworthy, that is, credible, generalizable, and dependable, rests mainly on the positionality of the researchers. The crux of discussions about trustworthiness across empirical research approaches center on whether other researchers, using the same methodology and similar participants, settings, and conditions, would produce reasonably comparable results. Of relevance to trustworthiness, the current researchers have dedicated much of their lives in professional and deeply personal ways to teaching, theorizing, researching, and building programs for African American college students and, more directly, Black men. We are Black, and we have an intimate relationship with the subject matter and to the participants, regardless of whether we knew any of them prior to the study, and most of us did not. We contend that it is our close proximity, desire for closeness, and emic approach

that makes the findings of the present study trustworthy and, indeed, unique. We suspect that another group of researchers without our theoretical lens, experience, commitment, and positionality would not yield the same findings. This is not biased research; rather, it is the essence of pure research in terms of knowing the other, which is the ability to see the world and phenomenon from the subjects' position. (Bush et al., 2022, pp. 255–266)

To conclude this chapter, we present an exercise adapted from an assignment given by Professor Michelle Foster in her qualitative research methods course many years ago, as well as from a practice by Dr. Carver. Dr. Carver would receive hundreds of letters from farmers seeking help with various agricultural issues. He would read the letters at night and then arise in the morning with the answers, stating that his subconscious would find the solutions while he slept. The exercise is designed to aid in the development of a researcher's emic perspective and provide a practice opportunity on seeing/hearing. Before that, we provide you with a list of strategies to sharpen or enlarge your methodological skills as a (re)searcher, that is a healer of Black boys and men. Remember that "enlarging one's vision and abilities has nothing supernatural about it, rather it is natural to be part of nature and to participate in a wider understanding of reality." In this light, engaging in the methods on the list is no different than a biologist adjusting a microscope to bring cells into sight, or an astronomer adjusting the lens of a telescope to bring objects into view that would otherwise go unseen. Similarly, it is akin to a quantitative researcher calibrating a survey instrument, or a qualitative researcher fine-tuning interview questions, or even turning up the power of a hearing aid to hear a dog whistle. In this case, you, the researcher, are the instrument.

## SCIENTIFIC METHODS TO ENHANCE A (RE)SEARCHER'S ABILITY TO GATHER DATA BY INCREASING ONE'S CAPACITY TO SEE AND HEAR PHENOMENA, MATTER, INTERACTIONS, AND DYNAMICS

- Participating in rituals like spirit baths, baptisms, and other sacred ceremonies
- Praying and fasting
- Being initiated into African spiritual systems
- Honoring and remembering your Ancestors
- Accessing the energy of the other Deities/Angels
- Spending time in Africa beyond tourist destinations
- Spending time with elders and children
- Meditating
- Spending time with people who have notable spiritual power
- Participating in group worship experiences particularly those more rooted in indigenous practices
- Gardening
- Remembering and studying words and scriptures of power
- Exercising and eating living foods
- Giving to and serving others
- Singing, dancing, and listening to divine music
- Practicing ritual sacrifice
- Using sacred medicines/plants
- Spending time with the ocean, rivers, creeks, mountains, and forests
- Living righteously with gratitude and gratefulness

## CONCLUDING EXERCISE

If you are an instructor of a course, have the students divide into groups of two. If you are working independently as a student or researcher, choose someone who does not live with you to assist you with this exercise. Have your partner (or the person you are working with, who is not in your class) take a picture of the seven most meaningful items in their living space. A few days later, visit your partner's living space and take seven pictures of what you believe are the most meaningful items to them. The night before your visit, write the person's name on a piece of paper and place it under your pillow before going to sleep. Meditate on it and ask to see what is important to your partner or participant. When you awaken, write down the seven items that you think you may see as meaningful to the other person. If this exercise is done in a class setting, the students can present their sets of pictures to the class along with the list of seven items they wrote down before visiting. If the exercise is done independently, have your participant send you their pictures to see how much they match with your set of pictures and your list. The more pictures that match your set of pictures and list, the greater your emic or insider's perspective, and perhaps your ability to see/hear.

# CHAPTER 4

## *The Sankofa (Re)search Model*

This chapter aims to provide readers with a clear and concise understanding of the vital components of the Sankofa (Re)search Model. As an important sidenote, we call our approach a model, as it is a broader term that encompasses both a research methodology—the "why"—and the method—the "how." To produce said understanding, we will provide readers with a breakdown of the axiology, ontology, methodology, and epistemology, along with the goals, aims, and objectives of the (re)search methodology. As we categorize each methodological component into various sections, it becomes important to note the overlay of several components of the (re)search methodology. For example, the notion of the (re)searcher being a healer will overlay in axiology and ontology. The malleability of these components reflects the nonlinear aspects of the methodology while simultaneously pushing back against binary approaches to research.

Malleability and elasticity are also located in AAMT's relevance and application to the (re)search methodology. AAMT informs every aspect of the Sankofa (Re)search Model and could easily be categorized within the axiology, ontology, methodology, and epistemology, along with the goals, aims, and objectives of the (re)search model. In fact, this work could easily be understood as the African American Male Theory's (Re)search Model. To overstate this point, a focus on a tenant of AAMT to approximate its centrality to the (re)search methodology may prove instructive. AAMT tenant c) There is a continuity and continuation of African culture, consciousness, and biology that influence the experiences of African American boys and men. The presence of Afrikan[1] culture, consciousness, and biology throughout the Sankofa (Re)search Model is pervasive; least we do not forget that Sankofa is a concept and symbol that derives from Afrika. The authors recognize the power of this Afrikan symbol and its ability to tap into the collective consciousness of Black boys and men, independent of their geographical and ideological relationship to Afrika. AAMT tenant c highlights the resounding presence of Afrika in all-Black boys and men, making the use of Afrikan symbolism not only logical but necessary. From an ontological standpoint, the Sankofa (Re)search Model advances the idea of Afrikan personhood, which directly aligns with AAMT tenant c. Hence, if Afrikan culture, consciousness, and biology influence Black boys and men's experiences, then it becomes imperative that a (re)search model for Black boys and men is grounded in an understanding of Afrikan personhood. Understanding Black boys and men to be anything other than Afrikan would produce inaccurate and irrational research.

As we move to the subsequent part of this section, we ask readers to be attentive to the overlap; think of this as an exercise in

---

[1]We spell Africa with a "C" and with a "K." Some scholars contend that Africans use the letter "K" in such words; Europeans polluted the spelling by switching the "K" to a "C" during the attempted colonization of the Afrikan continent, asserting that reverting to the "K" spelling empowered Afrikans and created the foundation for a shared identity between us.

pushing your thinking beyond the limitations of binary and linear conceptualizations of (re)search. We invite you, dear reader, to explore the boundless possibilities of free Black thought as you attempt to grapple with the components and their categorization. Black boys and men are not confined to binary or linear realities. As researchers of Black boys and men, we must avoid thinking and conducting research constrained by narrow perspectives. For readers who believe research must adhere to rigid guidelines and fit neatly into specific categories, it is crucial to recognize that such limitations do not capture the complexity of these lived experiences. We invite you to think critically about the research methodologies that come from Western thought. Do they not have elements of elasticity or overlay that can be found in multiple registries? We will investigate this line of thinking further in the concluding exercise. For now, we offer you a concise breakdown of the Sankofa (Re)search Model.

## SANKOFIC AXIOLOGY

*Axiology* refers to the researcher's understanding of values and their significance in research. It explores values, addresses questions of right and wrong, and evaluates the development and nature of perceptual biases.

The given definition of axiology properly centers on the importance of knowing a researcher's axiology to gain a deeper understanding of the research. Moreover, the given definition of axiology further authenticates our views of the (re)searcher's centrality to the (re)search process. We argued earlier that the researcher, the person, is the most significant component of the research process irrespective of the employed research paradigm or methodology. This emphasis on the researcher's role serves to make the audience feel their significance and impact. The axiology of the Sankofa (Re)search Model is grounded in the values detailed further.

Divine or ordained work is the foremost and central component of the Sankofa (Re)search Model as we posit in the opening chapter, "To operate in this capacity, you must see yourself in the likeness of God and that the post or position of researcher was ordained and sanctioned by God so that you can produce divine (re)search. This is achieved by a keen ability to listen or be a hearer of your participants, your wise ancestors, and God." This passage provides a perfect understanding of the magnitude and importance of this work. The value of the (re)searcher is located in the fact she is the likeness of God, and God has ordained her to conduct this (re)search. Hence, the role of the (re)searcher is to produce divine (re)search. Divine (re)search is intended to heal and (re)member Black boys and men, reassembling their bodies, restore them from the harm and disembodiment. To produce divine (re)search that will heal Black boys and men, the Sankofic (re)searcher must truly love Black boys and men. Not just loving them through the employment of the word, but a love that allows the (re)searcher to hear and see Black boys and men differently. Or more importantly as they truly are. The love for Black boys and men that must reside within the Sankofa (re)searcher should not only heal but propel the (re)searcher to (re)turn again and again, over and over to spend time with Black boys and men to uncover new truths about Black boys and men. Or as previously stated, "We are saying that a researcher of Black boys and men must operate in the Spirit of, or be possessed by, the spirit of Sankofa to produce divine words or narratives to heal Black boys and men." The Sankofa (re)searcher must not only speak words that are true, the (re)searcher must be trustworthy, able to establish a relevance and rapport with Black boys and men (Table 4.1).

**Table 4.1**   Sankofic Axiology

| Axiological Tenant | Descriptions |
| --- | --- |
| • Divine or Ordained work/Spiritual Practice | • To operate in this compacity, you must see yourself in the likeness of God and that the post or position of researcher was ordained and sanctioned by God so that you can produce divine (re)search. |
| • Healing Black boys and men | • In doing so, we position and delineate the role of the pedagogue in the ancient world as being the same role of a researcher, that is to heal. |
| • Loving Black boys and men | • "Anything will give up its secrets if you love it enough." |
| • Speaker of Truth upholders of MAAT | • (Re)searchers always speak the TRUTH. |
| • Producers of divine (re)search | • To produce mdw ntr or divine words pure, free, and decolonized Black thought, which we see as scripture and actions that liberate African people, particularly Black boys and men, causing them/us to reach their/our highest level of freedom and divinity. |
| • Relevance and rapport with Black boys and men | • It is the close proximity to Black boys and men, desire for closeness, and emic approach that makes the findings trustworthy. |

# SANKOFIC ONTOLOGY

*Ontology* is the philosophical study of being. It refers to your view of reality and to what extent it exists out there, to be captured through research. Ontology is concerned with what is true or real.

Like axiology, ontology is central to understanding any research methodology. The researcher's reality and their understanding of what exists "out there" will drastically shape the research process and outcomes. This is why we refuse to relinquish the biases inherited in the (re)searcher and (re)search process. AAMT proves to be instructive for highlighting how biases shape the (re)search process. AAMT tenant e) posits that race and racism coupled with classism and sexism have a profound impact on every aspect of the lives of African American boys and men. This tenant speaks to an ontological understanding of what exists "out there" for Black boys and men. Hence, the need for a (re)search model to heal and (re)birth Black boys and men from the harmful effects of racism, classism, and sexism. The authors know firsthand and with painstaking detail how race and racism, coupled with classism and sexism, have a profound impact on every aspect of the lives of Black boys and men. Our lived experiences as Black boys and men, coupled with the distinction we each hold as fathers of Black boys and men authenticate this claim. It is through this ontological positioning, and the deep recesses of free Black thought that this (re)search model is produced. It can be argued that it is through these biases that we are able to cultivate a (re)search model that understands the complex and nuanced plight of Black boys and men.

Like axiology, ontology is concerned with being. While axiology's interest in being is centered solely on the researcher, ontology's interest in being takes on a broader sense. However, in the context of this work, even from the ontological perspective, the focus on being shifts to Black boys and men, coupled with the (re)searcher. Consequently, you will see reoccurring themes and (re)search components restated throughout this section that were employed in the section on axiology. The reoccurring themes and restated (re)search components demonstrate the overlay and malleability stated at the start of the chapter. We offer you this disclaimer, dear reader, in an effort to avoid appearing redundant. We ask that you excuse any seeming redundancy as an attempt to be thorough and rigorous in our cultivation of this (re)search model. As previously mentioned, within the context of this project, ontology can be understood in two parts: (a) the (re)searcher and (b) Black boys and men. Table 4.2 offers readers a concise overview of some key ontological principles for both the Sankofic (re)searcher and Black boys and men.

Table 4.2    Sankofic Ontology

| Ontological Tenants: (Re)searcher | Descriptions |
|---|---|
| • Spiritual/Divine being | • To operate in this compacity, you must see yourself in the likeness of God and that the post or position of researcher was ordained and sanctioned by God so that you can produce divine (re)search. |
| • Healer | • In doing so, we position and delineate the role of the pedagogue in the ancient world as being the same role of a researcher, that is to heal. |
| • Educator | • The fact that a significant number of researchers are teachers today supports us making the appellation of teachers and researchers synonymous and to use them interchangeably. |
| • The ability to see/hear invisible entities | • All physical entities, including mountains, plants, trees, animals, bodies of water, and similar phenomena, contain spiritual energy, which is knowable to the individual who embodies or is spirit. |
| • The person is spirit | • All material objects are spiritual energy, including mountains, plants, trees, animals, bodies of water, and the like. |
| • The person is human | • The person is a living sun who, in human form, knows all that is spirit and has a relationship with the total perceptible and ponderable universe. |
| • There is no separation between matter, spirit, and the person | • Matter and the person exist simultaneously in the past, present, and future. |
| • The Zulu Personal Declaration | • The universes I challenge a higher being than me to show my knees do not quake when I contemplate my destiny. The eternal Person is Universal Man, Universal Woman, and Universal Child. |

# SANKOFIC METHODOLOGY

*Methodology* is a system of methods used in a particular study area or activity.

The methodology brings us to the nexus of this project. Axiology and ontology are vital as they help contextualize and quantify the work, but the methodology speaks to the systematic approach to accomplishing the work. To accomplish the work of (re)searching Black boys and men, the Sankofa (Re)search Model employs a variety of methods, foremost of which is the rigorous approach to (re)search. The Sankofic (re)searcher must be unrelenting in their approach to (re)search, willing to (re)turn again and again and again to engage Black boys and men. Sankofa embodies the notion of returning to retrieve the knowledge of the ancestors. We argue the Sankofa (re)searcher must be possessed by the spirit of Sankofa, willing to (re)turn and retrieve the knowledge held within Black boys and men and employ said knowledge in the production of divine free Black thought. To be possessed by the spirit of Sankofa to cultivate free Black thought is a drastic departure from Western approaches to research methods. The focal point of this particular (re)search methodology is that Black boys and men demand that we look not only at but beyond Westernized research methodologies, training, and qualitative/quantitative empirical measurement tools. One of the more harmful impacts research has had on the perception of Black boys and men is the reductionist perspective that seeks to paint Black boys and men as monoliths. Consequently, it would be nonsensical to employ monolithic and reductionist methodologies in the research of Black boys and men. While aspects of qualitative and quantitative methodologies will be found within this work, it becomes of great significance to note that the authors worked well beyond and were not limited to Westernized methodological approaches.

Working beyond Westernized methodological approaches does not preclude the authors from engaging in these methods. In fact, the use of quantitative research methods is not only central to the Sankofa (Re)search Model but is also a foundational aspect to Afrikan epistemological production. Moreover, we cannot assume for a moment that the people who founded mathematics, computation, and calculation did not engage in quantitative methods. In other words, we (re)claim quantitative methodology when employed in the context of the Sankofic (Re)search Model as indigenous Afrikan epistemology. As articulated in the previous chapter of this work, quantitative research, the practical application of the positivist paradigm employs numerical data collection and analysis methods to uncover patterns, relationships, and generalizable findings. This research model focuses on hypothesis testing, operationalization of variables, and controlled experimentation (McDougal, 2017). This passage highlights the use of numerical and data collection; the Ishango bone is the ideal personification of Afrikan people employing the use of numerical data collection. The evidence of the Ishango bone fortifies Afrika's ancient engagement with quantitative methodology. To engage in quantitative research methods is not a capitulation to Westernized methodological approaches. To engage in quantitative research methods within the framework of the Sankofic (Re)search Model is to employ divine ancient Afrikan intellectual technology. To engage in quantitative research methods within the framework of the Sankofic (Re)search Model is to (re)turn to the divine work of our ancestors, who sought to develop a greater understanding of their universe through the use of numerical computation. To foreclose quantitative methods from Afrika is to engage in deficit approaches to understanding Afrikan people, and for the Sankofic (re)searcher, to do so is antithetical to the desire of our (re)search model.

Within our attempts to "(re)claim quantitative methodology when employed in the context of the Sankofic (Re)search Model as indigenous Afrikan epistemology," it may prove instructive to theorize the importance of numbers within the framework of free Black thought. It is widely understood that numbers have an enormous impact and spiritual significance throughout Afrika. For divination and ancestral connection purposes, numbers are integral to Afrikan life experience. Within the Akan tradition, numbers are connected to certain taboos and misfortunes. Nana Akua K. Opokuwaa, in *The Akan Protocol: Remembering the Traditions of Our Ancestors* (2005), asserts,

> It is considered unlucky to give a person [five] 5 of anything. The number 5 in the Akan language sounds like the word "to regret." It is better to give a person four or six of something. If you really want to impress, give seven (7) of an object as it is supposed to be the ideal number. The Akan word [for seven] sounds like "to be sufficient" in the Akan language. Of course, there are other numbers that are desirable, which is a whole study. However, the main thing to remember about numbers is to never give five (5) of anything. (p. 135)

The point of this passage is not to point out how the number five is unlucky but to highlight the significance numbers play in Afrikan culture. However, as a sidenote, dissertations typically have five chapters; perhaps something to reconsider. Considering the centrality of numbers for Afrikan people, it becomes paramount that the Sankofa (Re)search Model engages numbers deeply. Numbers, like symbols, provide dynamic universal understanding within Afrikan epistemological production. Hilliard (1997) argues that "the symbol is the icon, of course, that carries many layers and levels of meaning" (p. 96). If we are to take the words of Hilliard to be accurate, then the Sankofic (re)searcher must engage numbers and the quantitative method with the understanding that they possess various layers and levels of meaning and the meaning must (re)store, (re)member, and (re)birth Black Boys and Men.

To engage in quantitative research methods within the framework of the Sankofic (re)search methodology is to employ divine ancient Afrikan intellectual technology. Engaging in quantitative research methods within the framework of the Sankofic (Re)search Model is to (re)turn to the divine work of our ancestors, who sought to develop a greater understanding of their universe through numerical computation. Numbers in Black-free thought function like how we have position Nature in this current text that is "to think of Nature as wireless telegraph stations through which God speaks to us every day, every hour, and every moment of our lives." In other words, numbers can be the conduit to carry messages or data from otherwise unseen phenomena. The Ifá divination system described in Chapter 3 gave us an example of this quantitative data-gathering method. Thus, to foreclose quantitative methods from Afrika is to engage in deficit approaches to understanding Afrikan people, and for the Sankofic (re)searcher, to do so is antithetical to the desire of our (re)search approach.

The essential need to push beyond Westernized research methodologies can be located in our rejection of deficit paradigm approaches to researching Black boys and men. Moving away from deficit paradigms allows for reimagining what success can look like for Black boys and men, identifying more robust opportunities for success beyond the status quo of careerism. Moreover, the rejection of deficit paradigms allows for the problematization of normative iterations of success by posing the following questions.

Which group of men, the men in prison or the men in college, would you define as successful? Can you imagine theorizing that Black boys and men in prison are more successful than those in college? Only liberated Black thought can guide you to the space for this theorized perspective. Keep in mind our new adage: Just because the lion is speaking, it doesn't mean he's not still telling the hunter's story. Much of the research on Black boys and men, predominantly conducted by Black men, can be classified as plantation scholarship—relying on colonial tools, frameworks, and methodologies to describe and reinforce life on the plantation. This approach ultimately upholds the existing asymmetrical power structures, rather than fostering a (re)search model aimed at achieving freedom and divinity.

Plantation scholarship/research has run its course. Scholarship/ (re)search that not only moves beyond the plantation but dismantles the plantation mentality is long overdue, which is why reimagining success is such a profound component of the Sankofa (Re)search Model. Success can no longer equate to surviving the plantation. Success must be measured by how one disrupts the functioning of the plantation or chooses death—specifically, death in the African sense, which is (re)birth—rather than acquiescing to the demands of plantation society.

We would like to (re)visit the emphasis on moving beyond Western methodologies for researching Black boys and men. Through a thorough investigation of Western research methodologies, the authors find storytelling and narrative (re)search approaches to align closest with our (re)search goals and aims. Narrative research consists of utilizing storytelling as a means of collecting data. As argued by Kim (2011) and Wells (2012), narrative research emphasizes the importance of contextual understanding, acknowledging the influence of cultural, social, historical, and personal factors shaping an individual's narrative. Researchers interpret and analyze narratives to identify underlying themes, patterns, and meaning. Engaging in the interpretation of narratives proves instructive for (re)searching Black boys and men, who possess an uncanny and unique capacity for narration and storytelling. Nevertheless, quintessential to narrative (re)search is the capacity of the (re)searcher to listen. However, to listen in the capacity that is required of the Sankofic (re)searcher, you must be able to listen with your heart, and to listen with your heart, you must love Black boys and men. To love Black boys and men unconditionally is vital to the production of free and pure Black thought, enabling the (re)searcher to view seeming flaws or shortcomings in Black boys and men as productive potential. To love Black boys and men is to have them reveal all their secrets to you. At the least, we should not forget Carver's contention, "Anything will give up its secrets if you love it enough." It is love that makes the immaterial material and allows the invisible to become visible. Thus, the vibration or energy of love has the capacity to position the person to hear/see matter or phenomena that might normally be undetectable by the physical eyes and ears. Hence, love is a prerequisite for (re)searching Black boys and men: granting access to the (re)searcher, data, or information that may not be detected otherwise, enhancing the ability to hear and see beyond the capabilities of the ears and eyes. Love, which stems from the heart, like a ritual, creates a particular vibrational dynamic that increases one's ability to see/ hear Spirit for data collection.

Like love, ritual is a critical component of the Sankofa (Re) search Model. Ritual is a ceremony, practice, or routine with the obligation to call in Spirit to guide, direct, speak, listen, or possess. The components and process of ritual allow the person to connect with other persons, Spirit, and Nature by removing barriers and blocks such as fears that stand between us and Spirit. In short, ritual is the act of communing with Spirit for guidance and direction. The practice of ritual as a (re)search methodology moves us further away from Westernized norms for research. However, while ritual moves us further away from the West, it places us in direct conversation with the Afrikan collective consciousness and the (re)search approach of George Washington Carver. As was mentioned in Chapter 3, Dr. Carver's ritual consisted of rising at 4 or 5 a.m. each day in the solitude of nature, and Dr. Carver had conversations with God, trees, plants, and rocks. In a dialogue with God, Dr. Carter asked, "Why did you make the peanut?" To this, God replied with a scientific plan: "Separate it into water, fats, oils, gums, resins, sugars, starches, and amino acids. Then recombine these under My three laws of compatibility, temperature, and pressure. Then you will know why I made the peanut." Carver's ritual or (re)search methodology was to rise before dawn, pray, and spend intimate time with the creator. This act of prayer and communion provided Carver with revelations and insight that drastically shaped his work.

Returning to a quote from Carver in Chapter 3, in which he posits, "My discoveries come like a direct revelation from God." Furthermore, he emphasized the intricate connection between nature and divine communication. These sentiments encapsulate his deep reverence for the natural world and a particular methodology for acquiring and advancing scientific knowledge and practice (Table 4.3).

Table 4.3   Sankofic Methodology

| Methodological Tenants | Descriptions |
| --- | --- |
| • Rigorous (Re)search | • Sankofa (re)searcher must be possessed by the spirit of Sankofa, willing to (re)turn and retrieve the knowledge held within Black boys and men and employ said knowledge in the production of divine free Black thought. |
| • Expand beyond the boundaries of Westernized methodologies | • Push beyond the boundaries of Westernized training and quantitative and qualitative empirical measurement tools. |
| • Quantitative Research Methods | • The Ishango bone is the ideal personification of the Afrikan people employing the use of numerical data collection. The evidence of the Ishango bone fortifies Afrika's ancient engagement with quantitative methodology…To engage in quantitative research methods within the framework of the Sankofic (Re)search Model is to employ ancient Afrikan intellectual technology. |
| • Rejection of deficit paradigm approaches and myopic frameworks | • Moving away from deficit paradigms allows for a reimagining of what success can look like for Black boys and men, identifying more robust opportunities for success beyond the status quo of careerism. |

| | |
|---|---|
| • Storytelling and Narrative Research | • Narrative inquiry, including oral histories, as a qualitative research methodology. |
| • Loving/Listening | • "Anything will give up its secrets if you love it enough." |
| • Ritual | • A ceremony, practice, or routine with the obligation to call in Spirit to guide, direct, speak, listen, or possess. The components and process of ritual allow the person to connect with other persons, Spirit, and Nature by removing barriers and blocks such as fears that stand between us and Spirit. |

# SANKOFIC EPISTEMOLOGY

*Epistemology* is the theory of knowledge, especially regarding its methods, validity, and scope. Epistemology is the investigation of what distinguishes justified belief from opinion.

Epistemology is the output of the (re)search methodology, the striving for mdw ntr (divine words) or divine free Black thought. However, epistemology is also the process of distinguishing justified belief from opinion and establishing the validity of the knowledge produced. As it pertains to the Sankofa (Re)search Model, the (re)searcher's proximity to Black boys and men allows for a clear distinction between justified belief and opinion. Hence, researching Black boys and men from a great distance increases the chances of producing research grounded in opinion as opposed to justified belief. The (re)searcher who operates in close proximity to Black boys and men not only increases the chances for (re)search grounded in justified belief but also increases the capacity for validity. A close proximity to Black boys and men allows for a trustworthy relationship between the (re)searcher and the subject to be (re)searched, ensuring the reliability of the research process. The established trustworthiness provides the pathway for valid (re)search, as it positions the information and data collected to be from a viable, knowledgeable, and trustworthy source, increasing not only the validity, but also the value of the information. Epistemology is also concerned with methods for knowing or knowledge, which recenters method, which also centers the spirituality of the (re)search process. Ritual is the ideal intersection of methods for knowing and spirituality. As previously mentioned, ritual is the ceremony of involving Spirit for guidance. Meditation, prayer, moments of deep contemplation, and conversations with God are all vital rituals that inform the epistemological process (Table 4.4).

**Table 4.4**   Sankofic Epistemology

| Epistemological Tenants | Descriptions |
|---|---|
| • The production of mdw ntr (divine words) | • Divine words distinguish belief from justified opinion. Justified opinion stems from divine words and truth. |
| • The production of valid and trustworthy knowledge | • The (re)searcher's proximity to Black boys and men is critical for the production of valid and trustworthy knowledge. |
| • Allowing ritual to produce forms of knowing | • Dr. Carver utilized an ancient African research or knowing method in the form of ritual as routine by arising and practicing prayer every day. |

# SANKOFIC GOALS, AIMS, AND OBJECTIVES

*The goals, aims, and objectives of the Sankofa (Re)search Model* are as dynamic and groundbreaking as the methodology itself. To (re)member, (re)store, and (re)birth Black boys and men is no small task. To heal Black boys and men is an endeavor that goes beyond the jurisdiction of any Westernized research methodology. It can easily be argued that the Sankofic (Re)search Model is the only research methodology and method that seriously examines the process of healing Black boys and men. To accomplish the goals, aims, and objectives of the (re)search methodology, every aspect of the axiology, ontology, methodology, and epistemology is integral. To (re)store is to resurrect Black boys and men. After (re)membering, it is the power of the researcher's words; this is the view that researchers aim to produce scripture, divine words, through positioning, analyzing, and theorizing in ways that breathes life and (re)stores. To (re)birth is to use the Sankofa (re)search approach, the act of looking and going back again and again as a guide to create or recreate or to birth or (re)birth new and free paradigms, language, and meaning as an act of worldmaking. To (re)store Black boys and men, the production of divine, true, decolonized Black thought becomes a necessary objective of the (re)search method. As we have previously stated, to produce mdw ntr or divine words— pure, free, and decolonized Black thought, that we see as scripture and actions that liberate African people, particularly Black boys and men, causes them/us to reach their/our highest level of freedom and divinity. Consequently, a foundational aim of this work is to bring out the divinity that may lay latent or dormant in Black boys and men (Table 4.5).

Table 4.5   Sankofic Goals, Aims, and Objectives

| Goals, Aims, and Objectives | Description |
| --- | --- |
| • (Re)store Black boys and men | • To (re)store is to resurrect Black boys and men. |
| • (Re)member Black boys and men | • To (re)member is to employ the power of the researcher's words; to produce scripture, divine words, through positioning, analyzing, and theorizing in ways that breathes life and (re)stores. |
| • (Re)birth Black boys and men | • To (re)birth is to use the Sankofa (re)search approach, the act of looking and going back again and again as a guide to create or recreate or to birth or (re)birth new and free paradigms, language, and meaning as an act of worldmaking. |

*(Continued)*

**Table 4.5** (Continued)

| Goals, Aims, and Objectives | Description |
|---|---|
| • Heal Black boys and men | • The Sankofic (re)search methodology is the only research methodology that takes a serious examination at the process of healing Black boys and men. |
| • The production of mdw ntr (divine words) | • To produce mdw ntr or divine words—pure, free, and decolonized Black thought, that we see as scripture and actions that liberate African people, particularly Black boys and men. |
| • Bring out the divinity in Black boys and men | • Consequently, a foundational aim of this work is to bring out the divinity that may lay latent or dormant in Black boys and men. |

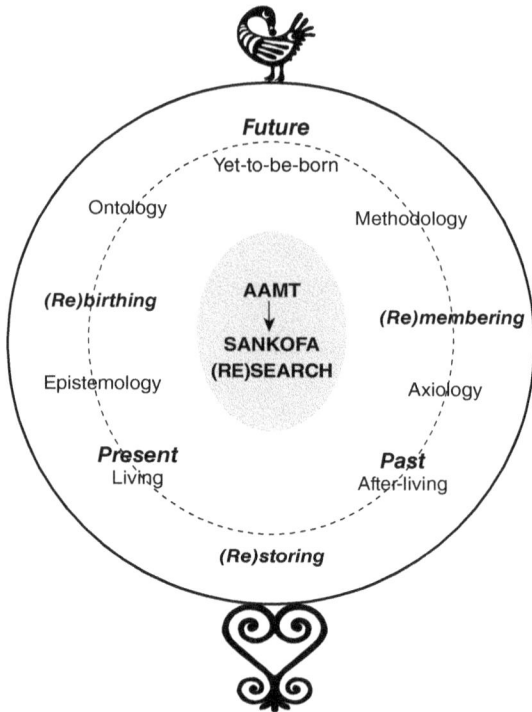

**Figure 4.1** Sankofa (Re)search Model 3.0

To further underscore the emphasis placed on the el\asticity, overlay, and cross-categorization of the Sankofa (Re)search Model, we provide Figure 4.1 to highlight not only the elasticity of the method but also the nonlinearity and the cyclical nature of the model, centering not only the axiology, ontology, methodology, epistemology but also the goals, aims, and objectives of the (re)search model. The image also highlights AAMT's centrality to the (re)search model while simultaneously situating Afrikan notions of temporal-linearity and the cyclical nature of past (afterlife), present (living), and future (yet-to-be-born) and how they all work in unison in the production of divine, decolonized, free Black thought.

## CONCLUDING EXERCISE

We invite you to (re)turn to the third chapter and (re)engage the various Westernized research methodologies, looking for the overlay or cross-categorizations found in each method's axiologies, ontologies, methodologies, and epistemologies. If located, does the overlay or cross-categorization found in Westernized research methods take away from their creditability or effectiveness? If you feel that it does not, ask yourself whether the overlay or cross-categorization in the Sankofa (Re)search Model takes away from its credibility or effectiveness? If you feel that it does, we ask that you (re)turn to the reflection question in Chapter 2: (If you fully embraced AAMT, how would this impact your practice and research approach?) Consider the tenants found in AAMT, then consider how they impacted your conceptualization of the (re)search methodology or the lack thereof. What complications prevent you from fully accepting the (re)search model we are advancing? However, suppose you feel that the elasticity, overlay, and cross-categorization of the

Sankofa (Re)search Model are generative but need to see the overlay and cross-categorization in the Westernized approaches to see the value in the Sankofa model. In that case, we ask you to contemplate the need to have the Westernized gaze justify Afrikan epistemological advancements.

# CHAPTER 5

## *From Model to Practice: Writing Divine Words and Applying the Sankofa (Re)search Model*

The culmination of any journey rooted in the Sankofa spirit requires reflection, (re)membering, and (re)storing the lessons gained along the way. This book has illustrated that the role of the researcher of Black boys and men is not only to document knowledge but to heal through that knowledge. The Sankofa principle, symbolized by the bird that looks back while holding an egg, reminds us that moving forward requires retrieval of the wisdom embedded in the past. This act aligns with the story of Ausar and Auset, where Auset's search for the scattered pieces of her husband represents the journey of a (re)searcher who gathers fragmented truths. Once reassembled, these truths empower individuals and communities to reclaim their wholeness.

In African cosmologies, "The Word" is sacred, and the act of speaking or writing carries the weight of creation itself. For example, recall from Chapter 1 that in the Kemetic tradition, mdw ntr is translated as "divine words." One story says that the God Ptah conceived the world in his heart and brought it to life through the power of his divine words. This idea also finds resonance in the New Testament from the Gospel of John, which declares: "In the beginning was the Word, and the Word was with God, and the Word was God" (John 1:1). These profound words affirm that creation and existence are fundamentally tied to language. "The Word," and considering what we have said about reclaiming quantitative methods previously, "The Number" are not merely symbols of communication or value; they are the embodiment of divine potential, forces capable of shaping reality.

For the (re)searcher guided by Sankofa, the sacredness of the Word becomes the cornerstone of their work, and in fact, as the scripture suggests, you become God-like. The (re)searcher who operates with this understanding is no longer engaging in the r(e) search intellectually, but as a spiritual practice, a process of co-creation with the ancestors, the divine, and the community. The Sankofic (re)searcher produces divine words (mdw ntr), scripture, and numbers conceived in a heart full of a profound love for Black boys and men to foster and create (re)search that (re) members, (re)stores, and (re)births.

This chapter explores the sacred dimensions of writing divine words and presents writing as a spiritual act that intertwines history, identity, spirit, responsibility, and accountability while also providing practical insights as to how to incorporate this approach within the mechanics of a dissertation and research paper. With this end mind, this chapter explores how to create a sacred space for writing, the role of the researcher, the power, purpose and responsibility of the researcher, and how this is captured in the writing of the literature review and the methodology.

## CREATING A SACRED WRITING PRACTICE

In Black church traditions, prior to the preacher delivering a sermon he/she will begin the sermon with a prayer/meditation that often will start with this scripture Psalm 19:14(KJV)

"Let the words of my mouth, and the meditation of my heart, be acceptable in thy sight, O Lord, my strength, and my redeemer." This practice is rooted in the idea that the preacher as a person will be moved out of the way to make space for the Holy Spirit to step in to speak through the preacher to deliver a message directly from God with the intention to "save" or to "deliver" the congregation by providing a word that would speak to their current condition. Likewise, a (re)searcher rooted in the Sankofa practice begins with intentionally creating a space where the spirit can overtake the (re)searcher as a person and replace it with the Holy Spirit to address the conditions of Black boys and men. This practice allows the (re)searcher to create internal and external space that serves as both a literal and metaphorical sanctuary, enabling the (re)searcher to engage with the work fully. Just as African ancestors would prepare sacred spaces for rituals, (re)searchers can design environments that honor the sacred nature of their writing. This may involve surrounding oneself with objects of personal significance—such as photographs of ancestors, spiritual symbols, and books that have shaped one's journey. Many (re)searchers adopt rituals that mark the transition from everyday life into sacred writing time. Lighting candles, burning sage, or engaging in breathwork before writing helps to clear the mind and create focus. African spiritual traditions often emphasize music and rhythm, which can also become essential elements of a sacred writing practice. (Re)searchers might dance, listen to hip-hop, gospel, jazz, or traditional drumming to enter a creative flow state, mirroring the way rhythm in African traditions connects individuals with deeper states of consciousness.

The ritual of invoking ancestors not only grounds the (re)searcher in historical consciousness but also fosters a sense of spiritual guidance. Building an ancestral altar in the writing space, offering libations, or praying before writing sessions creates a spiritual connection to the wisdom of those who came before. These practices embody the spirit of Sankofa by acknowledging that the work is not produced in isolation but draws upon collective histories and ancestral knowledge.

Furthermore, fasting, meditation, and physical exercise align the (re)searcher with the spiritual demands of sacred writing. In many traditions, fasting symbolizes purification—a clearing away of distractions to allow for clarity and insight. This practice parallels the (re)searcher's need to set aside internalized white practices and make space for inspiration and unanticipated revelations. Physical exercise, such as yoga or walking meditations, supports emotional balance and mental clarity, ensuring that the (re)searcher remains grounded throughout the writing process.

Incorporating these practices into the writing routine nurtures both the body and the spirit, reminding the (re)searcher that writing divine words requires holistic preparation. It transforms writing from a task into a devotional practice, cultivating an atmosphere where inspiration flows freely.

## PREACHABLE WORDS: TRANSCENDING ACADEMIC BOUNDARIES

In conversations with fellow (re)searchers who are rooted in AAMT, it is often asked if what is written is "preachable." This means that we are able to translate what is written on paper to transcend into another dimension where the words can flow enough to move the people. The concept of preachabilty is directly tied to what we have outlined about the Sankofic (re)searcher being a producer of scripture, mdw ntr, and divine numbers. Therefore, we look for the opportunity to preach our (re)search and writing to test whether what we wrote resonates and penetrates the hearts and minds of Black people. One can imagine that this is the same process for a hip-hop artist or a spoken words artist where they are not writing with the intention for it to sound good on paper, but they are writing with the intention of how their writing will move the people or in other words how it would preach. Within a Black context, how you say it is tantamount to what you say, and given that Black people are multidimensional beings, the words of the (re)searcher also need to resonate multi-dimensionally. Preachable words are those that transcend intellectual understanding, engaging the heart, soul, and spirit of the audience. They draw upon the rhythms of spoken word, story-telling, and poetry to evoke emotional responses. This form of writing bridges the gap between academia and lived experience, making research accessible and impactful across multiple contexts.

In writing preachable words, (re)searchers must be intentional about their language, choosing resonating metaphors and imagery. Such writing does not shy away from vulnerability; it embraces it, inviting readers to connect deeply with the work. These words are designed to be shared in classrooms, churches, healing circles, and public protests, creating spaces for reflection and action. With this in mind, the authors encourage you to practice reading your research out loud, asking others to read your words out loud, feeling how the words set on your spirit, and gauging the energy provoked when the words are read. If the words move you and the spirit, then it is an indication of the power and impact of your writing.

Preachable words also inspire action. They carry the potential to mobilize communities and catalyze change. In this way, the (re)searcher becomes a griot—a storyteller who preserves history while inspiring future possibilities. (Re)search becomes a living force, transforming the spaces it touches and contributing to the healing of those it seeks to serve.

## THE (RE)SEARCHER'S ROLE IN THE STRUGGLE FOR LIBERATION

The tradition of Black authorship, from Frederick Douglass to Toni Morrison, teaches us that words can be instruments of change. Writing is not neutral. Scholars committed to liberating Black boys and men must understand that their work participates in the broader struggle for justice rooted in love. Like educators and healers, (re)searchers must produce knowledge that disrupts systems of oppression and inspires transformative action. Below are some additional voices that positioned (re) search as a tool of liberation grounded in love:

- W.E.B. Du Bois, one of the most influential Black scholars of the 20th century, used his research to affirm the humanity of Black people and challenge the racial hierarchies of his time. His groundbreaking sociological study The Philadelphia Negro (2010) was motivated by his love for Black people and a desire to counter the dehumanizing stereotypes that prevailed in American society.

- Ella Baker, a key organizer in the Civil Rights Movement, embodied love as the foundation of her work by centering community-driven leadership.

- bell hooks, the cultural critic and feminist theorist, articulated the power of love as a political force in her writings. She argued that love was essential to dismantling systems of domination and creating transformative communities. In her work, hooks often highlighted the importance of seeing oneself in others as a pathway to liberation.

- Malcolm X, though often remembered for his fiery rhetoric, was deeply motivated by a love for Black freedom and dignity. His speeches and writings reflect a profound respect for the self-determination and sovereignty of Black people, grounded in his belief in the transformative power of knowledge and self-awareness.

- In this light, our role as (re)searchers extends beyond academic spaces. Knowledge must transcend institutional boundaries, resonating within communities where it can foster liberation. Public presentations, community workshops, and digital platforms are avenues through which (re)search can reach and empower broader audiences. In this way, (re)search becomes praxis—a process in which knowledge inspires reflection, conversation, and action within the community. Moreover, this role demands intentionality. (Re)searchers must ask themselves: Whose voices are centered in this work? How does this research disrupt systems of inequality? What tangible impact will this work have on the community? These questions ensure that the research aligns with the broader mission of liberation.

Research on Black boys and men, for instance, has historically been conducted from a deficit-oriented perspective, reducing them to objects of study and framing their experiences through the lens of pathology and failure. The insistence on neutrality has too often meant erasing the humanity of both the researcher and the researched, perpetuating narratives that fail to account for these communities' brilliance, resistance, resilience complexity, and cultural richness.

The pursuit of objectivity has also reinforced systemic inequities within the research process. Traditional methodologies often privilege Eurocentric perspectives by discouraging researchers from engaging with their cultural identities and lived experiences, rendering other epistemologies invisible or invalid. The erasure of the researcher's identity becomes, in effect, a replication of the erasure of Black communities, perpetuating epistemic violence and reinforcing existing power structures.

AAMT and the Sankofa (Re)search Model challenge these limitations, offering a paradigm that explicitly integrates the (re)searcher's lived experience, identity, and cultural context into the (re)search process. This approach begins with the acknowledgment that all research is inherently situated—that is, it emerges from specific historical, cultural, and social contexts that shape both the researcher and the researched. Far from being a source of bias, the researcher's positionality is understood as a lens through which knowledge is generated, interpreted, and applied.

In this model, the (re)searcher is not an impartial observer but a deeply engaged participant whose voice is central to the work. The lived experiences of the (re)searcher—shaped by their identity, cultural background, and personal journey—become vital tools for inquiry. These experiences allow the (re)searcher to connect with the subject matter more profoundly, enabling them to ask more meaningful questions, interpret data with greater nuance, and produce findings that resonate with the realities of the communities they study.

For example, a researcher who has navigated systemic racism in educational institutions brings a distinct perspective to studies on Black boys in schools. Their lived experience equips them to recognize patterns of inequity, understand the cultural contexts of resistance and resilience, and critically interrogate the structures that perpetuate racism and white supremacy. This connection does not compromise the rigor of their work; rather, it enhances it, providing insights that are often inaccessible to researchers who approach the subject from a position of detachment.

## CULTURAL AUTHENTICITY AS A (RE)SEARCH IMPERATIVE

The Sankofa (Re)search Model builds on the African philosophical principle of *ubuntu*, which asserts that an individual's humanity is inextricably linked to the humanity of others. This interconnectedness positions the researcher not as an outsider but as a member of their study community, bound by shared histories, struggles, and aspirations. Honoring cultural authenticity, therefore, becomes a central imperative of the (re)search process. The (re)searcher's cultural identity and experiences are not incidental; they are essential to producing ethically and epistemologically grounded work.

Cultural authenticity also fosters a sense of accountability. In traditional models of neutrality, researchers are often absolved of responsibility for the impact of their work on the communities they study. The Sankofa approach, by contrast, demands that (re)searchers consider the ethical implications of their work, ensuring that it serves the interests of those it seeks to understand. This accountability is particularly critical concerning the (re)search on Black boys and men, where the stakes are high, and the consequences of misrepresentation can be profound.

Integrating lived experience into the (re)search process is not rejecting rigor but expanding it. The Sankofa (Re)search Model requires (re)searchers to engage in ongoing self-reflection, examining how their positionality shapes their perspectives and interpretations. This practice is not about imposing personal narratives on the work but about using them as a lens to illuminate hidden dimensions of the subject matter.

In this framework, positionality becomes a source of insight rather than bias. It allows (re)searchers to approach their work with empathy, humility, and a deeper understanding of the complexities of human experience and, thus, Black men and boys. By acknowledging their subjectivity, (re)searchers can engage more honestly with the subjectivity of their participants, creating a (re)search process that is collaborative, reciprocal, and transformative.

Incorporating lived experience also transforms the (re)search relationship, positioning it as a partnership rather than a hierarchical exchange. In traditional research paradigms, participants are often treated as subjects to be studied, their voices filtered through the detached interpretations of the researcher, and as is often the case with studies on Black boys and men where researchers view them as the problem in the room that needs to be fixed. The Sankofa model disrupts this dynamic, emphasizing the co-creation of knowledge. Participants are invited to share their stories in their voices, and their insights are treated as integral to the (re)search process.

This collaborative approach not only enhances the quality of the (re)search but also contributes to its healing potential. When participants see their experiences validated and honored, they are empowered to reclaim their narratives and assert their agency. Similarly, the (re)searcher benefits from the reciprocal exchange of knowledge, deepening their understanding and strengthening their commitment to the work.

By honoring lived experience and authenticity, the Sankofa (Re) search Model redefines what it means to produce rigorous and impactful (re)search. This paradigm does not discard the principles of accountability and critical inquiry; instead, it elevates them, rooting them in a framework that values interconnectedness, cultural context, and the humanity of both the researcher and the researched.

This approach challenges (re)searchers to bring their whole selves to their work—to acknowledge their histories, identities, and passions as vital elements of the (re)search process. It calls for an intellectually robust scholarship that is spiritually and emotionally resonant, producing knowledge that heals, (re) stores, and liberates. By rejecting the myth of neutrality and embracing the power of authenticity, the Sankofa (Re)search Model offers a transformative vision for the future of (re) search—one that honors the humanity of Black men and boys.

# WRITING A LITERATURE REVIEW USING THE SANKOFA FRAMEWORK

A literature review in the Sankofa framework transforms from a mere synthesis of existing knowledge to an act of (re)membering, where historical truths are reclaimed, lived experiences are honored, and healing narratives are constructed. This approach requires a deliberate departure from traditional, detached reviews and embraces writing as an offering that uplifts and restores.

The Sankofa framework reframes the literature review as a sacred act of gathering wisdom from the past to inform the present and future. (Re)searchers are not simply documenting prior studies; they are engaging in the deliberate retrieval of marginalized knowledge and the elevation of voices often erased in traditional scholarship. By centering African and Black epistemologies, the literature review becomes a tool for justice and empowerment.

The following excerpt from a short fictional story by McDougal (2020b) entitled *The Africology Imagination in Nocturne: Dreams of Sitting at the Table of Obaba: Unity, and the Come-Unity Line* embodies many of the components stressed in the Sankofa (Re)search Model, including the invoking of the ancestors as guides for your work, in addition to demonstrating some of the basic mechanics of writing a literature review positioning it as a dialogue between important authors and paramount concepts that are woven together to tell a particular story or to uncover and build a particular perspective. However, the voice of the (re)searcher, or in the case of the excerpt below, the storyteller, is not lost or pretends to be hidden, which is a characteristic of other research paradigms; instead, the voice of the Sankofic (re)searcher is seen as central to the (re)search process and the writing of a literature review. Above all things, we hope that the short story puts the reader in the space of imagining and feeling what we mean when we say that writing a literature review from the Sankofic model is a sacred act of gathering wisdom from the past to inform the present and future. In fact, it is a ritual.

*As I sat at home, I noticed that I had just been sitting there, alone, thinking about unity for nearly an hour. I continued, since it was better than going on a YouTube bender. I had my back against one of the four walls in my studio apartment, and the other three were covered by bookcases. As I sat against the empty wall, I could see the titles of the books on each shelf. With unity on my mind, certain books jumped out at me, until I could see the authors surrounding my bed.*

*I'd had strong waking dreams like this many times before, but there was always something in me that resisted falling too deep into the dream. I dismissed them as daydreaming, a waste of time. I would tighten my muscles to avoid losing control at these times out of fear of what unknown state my mind might enter. This time, however, I let go; I let whatever was happening happen.*

*What happened was that the Obaba surrounded me, the ancestral presences of Marcus Garvey, Frantz Fanon, Kwame Ture, Wade Nobles, Martin Luther King, Louis Farrakhan, and Malcolm X. I was frozen in shock! I felt inappropriate in every way: mentally unprepared, underdressed. I didn't even have any shoes on ... in the presence of Malcolm X, for crying out loud. Of all things, I was wondering how Dr. Nobles and Minister Farrakhan could be there, since they were still alive.*

*I looked around my bed in awe at their faces looking back at me. But then, I was taken aback by the fact that Fanon was staring at me with one eye half-closed and the other wide open. Good lord! Was this man trying to look into my soul? He seemed to have a stronger connection to me than the others at that moment. Fanon sat with his legs crossed and his hands folded over his knee. Still looking directly at me, he said, "He's wondering about Brother Wade and Minister Farrakhan." He was right.*

*Dr. Nobles spoke next, saying, "You teach Africana Studies correct? Don't you know we are all spirit in a physical body, having a human experience? Have I not taught you that I can spiritually be in more than one place at the same time?" He was right! Ancestral souls return all the time in newborns, yet they don't lose their place in the ancestral realm. What was I thinking? It made sense.*

*Minister Farrakhan, wearing his tinted glasses and a yellow suit, leaned forward to speak. He said, "I know this is a confusing and perhaps even frightening experience in your life, so I greet you in the name of Allah, the beneficent, the merciful. I bear witness that there is no God but Allah and I bear witness that Muhammad is his messenger. Brother…you are here because of the importance of unity; your spirit led you to the question of unity. Dear brother, what the Black people need is not genius; we have plenty of that, as our people are as brilliant as ever. I am not sure it is even money; we have plenty of sources of capital. What we need is to connect the dots. Your spirit is right to focus on unity because our true capabilities cannot be realized without it. And, of course, we cannot depend on the benevolence of others. The responsibility is ours."*

*Swaying back and forward in his chair with his eyes half closed, Kwame Ture responded, "Yes, I agree, because I believe that united, people of African descent are the most powerful people in the world. But for a revolutionary, Minister Farrakhan, it is my understanding that the most important part of a revolution is the people's consciousness as I've said before. I say this to you, brothers, because in our talk about unity, I wonder if we are not putting the cart before the horse. This country tries to instill within our people a false consciousness, to make you accept its lies and go about living those lies."*

*"That's true: nationalism happens along with the raising of awareness of consciousness, as you put it, Brother Kwame," Frantz Fanon interjected. "Unity of consciousness is essential; in fact, individualism must be the first thing to disappear in a revolution. Individualism is the mantra taught by the oppressor, and unity is the antidote to the cancer of individualism. It must be maintained through political education of the masses. This is what you have to do, professor."*

# COMPARING TRADITIONAL VERSUS SANKOFA-ALIGNED LITERATURE REVIEWS

A Sankofa-aligned literature review differs significantly from traditional approaches:

- *Purpose*: Traditional reviews often aim to identify gaps in the literature to justify the research. Sankofa reviews focus on reclaiming erased histories, healing fragmented narratives, and constructing a framework for liberation.
- *Scope*: Traditional reviews rely heavily on peer-reviewed articles and established theoretical frameworks. Sankofa reviews draw on a broader range of sources, including oral traditions, spiritual texts, and cultural artifacts, emphasizing depth and cultural authenticity.
- *Tone*: Traditional reviews often maintain a detached, neutral tone. Sankofa reviews are intentionally engaged, viewing the (re) searcher as an active participant in the restoration of knowledge.

# ORGANIZING THE LITERATURE

Effective organization is vital for ensuring that the literature review reflects the Sankofa framework. (Re)searchers can categorize sources based on thematic relevance, methodological alignment, or historical significance:

1. *Chronological and Thematic Structure:*
   - Present older, foundational works first, followed by more recent studies.
   - Identify how these works contribute to understanding the strengths and challenges faced by Black boys and men.

2. *Critique of Deficit Narratives:*
   - Deliberately identify and challenge works that frame Black boys and men through deficit-based perspectives.

- Debunk and resist that idea of creating a counternarrative as affirm Black history, culture, traditions, and lived experiences as an independent story that does not exist only in response to whiteness.

3. *Rejection of Mainstream Frameworks:*
   - Push back against the overreliance on mainstream theoretical frameworks such as CRT that center Blackness only in relation to whiteness, enslavement, or colonization.
   - Instead, utilize frameworks like Black Futurism, which imagines Black life beyond the confines of historical oppression, envisioning worlds where Black people control their destinies and thrive in self-determined spaces. For example, literature could explore Afrofuturist themes in education, where Black boys and men innovate freely without systemic constraints.
   - Prioritize sources authored by scholars from Black and African communities.
   - Incorporate oral histories, personal narratives, and nontraditional forms of knowledge. For example, including testimonies from community elders about indigenous healing practices provides a richer understanding of resilience and cultural continuity.

## CRITICAL ANALYSIS THROUGH SANKOFA

To analyze literature critically, (re)searchers must interrogate how studies align with or diverge from the principles of the Sankofa framework. Key questions include the following:

- Does this study recognize the cultural and historical context of Black boys and men?
- How does the work contribute to healing and liberation?

- Does the framework of this study imagine Blackness beyond oppression, fostering an aspirational and liberated future?
- What are the gaps, and how can the (re)searcher's work fill them?

By embedding these practices, the literature review becomes a powerful act of restoration and a foundation for transformative (re)search. It moves beyond documentation to envision a world where Black boys and men thrive in alignment with their cultural and historical heritage, free from the constraints of deficit-oriented paradigms.

## APPROACHING THE METHODOLOGY CHAPTER USING THE SANKOFA FRAMEWORK

The methodology chapter, as guided by the Sankofa framework, is not simply a technical explanation of research methods but a deliberate invocation of cultural authenticity and healing that (re)stores and (re)births. This section outlines how to apply the framework for both quantitative and qualitative studies.

### Foundations for Methodological Alignment

The Sankofa framework insists on situating methodology within cultural and historical contexts. This involves the following:

1. Positionality Statement:
   - Reflect on the (re)searcher's lived experiences, cultural background, and motivations.
   - Acknowledge how this shapes the choice of methods and the interpretation of findings.

2. Ethics of Care and Accountability:
   - Ensure that methods honor the dignity and agency of participants.
   - Commit to reciprocal relationships where participants benefit from the (re)search.

## APPLYING THE SANKOFA MODEL TO QUALITATIVE (RE)SEARCH

1. Methods:

   - Narrative inquiry, participatory action research, oral histories, and ethnography align well with the Sankofa model.
   - Example: Collect oral histories of Black boys' experiences in education, focusing on their resilience and aspirations.

2. Participant Engagement:

   - Create culturally affirming spaces for dialogue, incorporating practices such as storytelling or oral history collection.
   - Use practices like libations or invoking ancestors during interviews to honor cultural traditions.

3. Data Collection:

   - Healing and culturally responsive and situated focus groups.
   - Healing and culturally responsive and situated interviews.
   - Healing and culturally responsive and situated observations.

Under the Sankofa (Re)search Model, the site or place of gathering data should simultaneously serve as a site of healing for the (re)searcher and the participants. In the case of studying Black women, the healing aspect of women and friend groups gathering together as a support mechanism dates back to antiquity (Jones et al., 2023). However, framing these circles as sites for research—and, more specifically, as a (re)search approach—is a more recent concept and practice. Similarly, in modern times, the barbershop has been a space for dialogue and healing for Black men (Mills, 2004, 2005). Although the barbershop has been a place of scholarly inquiry and has been recognized by scholars as a healing space (Shabazz, 2016; Soares et al., 2024; Wippold et al., 2024), it has not been positioned or conceptualized as a research method.

In thinking about the barbershop as a (re)search approach, one should aim to recreate its dynamics and atmosphere when gathering data with Black boys and men. The barbershop provides freedom to express oneself authentically, outside of the gaze of "the other." Yet, while the barbershop is a site of healing and dialogue, it is also a site of challenge. Thus, how the (re)searcher moves, speaks, and even dresses—even details such as shoes or a watch—cannot be overlooked. These seemingly small matters and details can quickly render one an outsider or even unqualified. Above all, a Sankofic (re)searcher must be authentic, as Black boys and men have an uncanny ability to detect discrepancies in authenticity. You must strike a balance: being knowledgeable and worthy of respect, yet not projecting superiority or being untouchable.

Furthermore, you must demonstrate genuine interest in participants and convey that you have their best interests in mind—not from the perspective of having all the answers, but rather as someone who can collaboratively explore solutions or new concepts. Engage in conversations that explain who you are, what you do, and why the (re)search matters to Black boys and men. Also, ask them questions beyond the focus of your (re)search. If you are conducting focus groups or interviews with Black boys, keep in mind that, like most children, they have had limited exposure to a researcher, and likely almost none who work from a Sankofic (Re)search Model. Where appropriate, be explicit with Black boys and men about your positionality and approach within the Sankofic framework, much like what we advocate for in writing about your (re)search.

Building on Sistah circles and barbershop conversations, the Sankofic qualitative data collection model has the capacity to merge informal and formal therapy with data collection. This approach is being employed by Simmons (2025) in her work with Black women with lupus through art therapy as a focus group. Participants will work with clay, an ancient African practice, as a form of therapy while the (re)searcher collects data during the process. However, it is not a requirement of the Sankofa approach that formal therapy and data collection occur simultaneously. Instead, it is essential that the possibilities of healing and data collection coexist. Thus, interviews, focus groups, and observations should be rooted in ritual. Meditation, music, burning incense, libations, prayers, drumming, stretching, yoga, and creating art are all cultural healing elements that can be incorporated into data collection.

Finally, while the barbershop is described as a site of healing and dialogue for Black men and boys, it can also be a space of challenge—not only for the researcher who may lack authenticity but also between the barber and clients, as well as among clients themselves. The Sankofa (Re)search Model aims to foster such authentic spaces where Black boys and men feel free to challenge one another and even the (re)searcher. These exchanges are positioned as healthy, healing, and authentic, thus producing more reliable data.

1.  Data Analysis:
    *   Analyze data through thematic analysis while remaining grounded in cultural and historical contexts.
    *   Use African-centered coding frameworks that emphasize themes of identity, spirituality, and liberation.

## APPLYING THE SANKOFA (RE)SEARCH MODEL TO QUANTITATIVE (RE)SEARCH

QuantCrit is an emerging field of quantitative research that combines or infuses CRT and quantitative methods to call for a new quantitative analysis that centralizes race and racism (Arellano, 2022; Castillo & Babb, 2024). Moreover, it challenges the reductionist's tendency to reduce human beings to numbers. To that end, these scholars argue that numbers do not speak for themselves. Rather, they have to be explained and interpreted from a political/racialized, historical, and cultural context. We somewhat align with this emerging view about quantitative approaches and see QuantCrit as an amiable current in our push to reclaim quantitative practices under the umbrella of free Black thought. However, the Sankofa (Re)search Model pushes significantly further than the limited usage of numbers as a tool to combat racism, which is often expressed in deficit paradigms and constructs. Instead, we look at our ancestral and current indigenous cultural and spiritual practices to reposition our understanding of what numbers mean or represent. This means that we are looking at numbers as a means to expand rather than reduce. In this light, numbers are part of nature used to tell us a sacred and divine message.

## DATA COLLECTION: INSPIRATION FROM IFÁ DIVINATION

Again, as briefly covered in Chapter 3, in Ifá divination, a Babalawo (priest or diviner) uses sacred tools such as ikín (palm nuts) or an opele (divination chain) to engage with the sacred codes, or Odu, which form the core of Yoruba cosmology. Each of the 256 Odu contains a wealth of narratives, proverbs, and guidance that address various aspects of life, from personal struggles to communal issues (Karenga, 1999). The process involves invoking spiritual insight, engaging with symbolic representations, and interpreting results through a holistic lens that integrates material, emotional, and spiritual dimensions. Essentially as we have articulated in various ways, in the Sankofic paradigm, you, the (re)searcher, are the Babalawo, diviner/seer, and healer.

## KEY FEATURES OF IFÁ IN PRACTICE

1. Layered Meaning and Contextualization:
   - The Odu revealed during a divination session does not stand alone; it is deeply contextualized within the practitioner's lived reality. The Babalawo, or the (Re) searcher, interprets its meaning through oral traditions, spiritual knowledge, and relational understanding.

2. Interconnectedness:
   - Ifá emphasizes the interconnection between the individual, community, and cosmos. The insights provided are never isolated; they reflect a broader system of balance and reciprocity.

3. Active Participation:
   - Divination, or (re)search, is not a passive process. The individual seeking guidance actively participates by asking questions, reflecting, and engaging with the interpretations provided by the Babalawo or (re)searcher.

## TRANSLATING IFÁ PRINCIPLES INTO (RE)SEARCH DATA COLLECTION

(Re)searchers can adapt these features to design culturally resonant tools for data collection. Drawing on the depth and interconnectedness of Ifá, (re)searchers might create instruments that capture the complexity of participants' lived experiences. Examples:

1.  Multidimensional Surveys:
    *   Develop questions that address both material realities (e.g., access to resources, educational opportunities) and spiritual well-being (e.g., feelings of purpose, community connection).
    *   Example: A survey might ask participants to reflect on how their cultural values influence their personal goals, paralleling Ifá's integration of personal and cosmic alignment.

2.  Narrative-Informed Questions:
    *   Inspired by Odu narratives, include open-ended questions that allow participants to share stories or metaphors that resonate with their experiences.
    *   Example: "Describe a moment when you felt most aligned with your community's values. What did that teach you about your path forward?"

3.  Symbolic Data Gathering:
    *   Use culturally symbolic tools, such as images, proverbs, or artifacts, to elicit deeper insights during data collection. Participants might respond to visual prompts or symbols that connect to themes of resilience or balance.

4.  Iterative Dialogues:
    *   Like Ifá consultations, data collection can involve iterative dialogues where participants reflect on and expand their responses. This approach ensures their narratives are layered and contextualized.

By embedding the richness and complexity of Ifá into data collection methods, (re)searchers not only gather information but also honor participants' full humanity. This practice reflects the Sankofa framework's commitment to cultural authenticity, reciprocity, and transformative knowledge creation.

1. *(Re)search Design:*
   - Ensure quantitative studies address questions that affirm the humanity and strengths of Black boys and men.

2. *Numbers in African Contexts:*
   - Draw on practices such as the Dogon's use of numerical symbolism in their cosmology, where numbers explain celestial phenomena and cycles, illustrating how knowledge of the universe intertwines with spirituality.
   - Incorporate examples from Kemet (ancient Egypt), where precise measurements like the cubit were used in constructing pyramids, reflecting both mathematical mastery and alignment with cosmic principles.

3. *Data Collection:*
   - Use surveys and instruments designed or adapted for cultural relevance.
   - Engage with community-based participatory approaches to ensure tools reflect cultural values and lived experiences.
   - Relate these practices to the ritualistic gathering of data in African traditions, such as using rhythmic patterns to convey coded messages or engage with community narratives.

4. *Data Analysis:*
   - Frame quantitative results within the holistic African worldview where balance, harmony, and reciprocity are central themes.
   - Example: Correlate findings on educational interventions with African traditions of communal success, showing how programs improve outcomes for both individuals and their communities.

- Connect statistical outcomes to cultural metaphors—
  for example, seeing high success rates in mentorship
  programs as akin to a well-tended crop yielding abun-
  dance, an image deeply resonant in African agrarian
  traditions.

## INTEGRATING MIXED METHODS

The Sankofa framework encourages blending quantitative and
qualitative approaches to provide a holistic understanding. For
instance:

- Use surveys to measure the impact of interventions, supple-
  mented by in-depth interviews to capture lived experiences.
- Incorporate participatory data analysis sessions where participants help interpret findings, ensuring cultural
  authenticity and relevance.

## APPLYING THE FRAMEWORK IN
## METHODS AND DISCUSSION

The methods and discussion sections are where the (re)searcher
demonstrates the transformative potential of their work. Guided
by Sankofa, these chapters articulate how the (re)search process
contributes to healing, empowerment, and liberation.

Methods Section: Practical Applications

1. *Designing the (Re)search Process:*
   - Incorporate rituals such as pre-(re)search meditations or
     invoking ancestors to ground the work.
   - Create spaces—both physical and metaphorical—that
     honor cultural traditions and foster trust.

2. *Engaging Participants:*
   - Co-create the (re)search agenda with participants, ensuring their voices shape the process.
   - Use culturally affirming practices, such as storytelling or art-based methods, to gather data.

3. *Data Analysis Techniques:*
   - Approach analysis as an act of (re)membering, where fragmented histories and truths are reassembled.
   - Incorporate participant feedback into interpretations to ensure authenticity and relevance.

## Discussion Section: Framing the Implications

1. *Connecting Findings to Historical and Cultural Contexts:*
   - Situate findings within broader narratives of Black resilience and creativity.
   - Example: Link educational successes of Black boys to historical traditions of knowledge-sharing in African communities.

2. *Highlighting Contributions to Healing:*
   - Frame findings as tools for addressing systemic inequities and fostering individual and collective well-being.
   - Example: Show how culturally affirming practices can mitigate the impacts of intergenerational trauma.

3. *Offering Pathways for Action:*
   - Translate findings into actionable recommendations for educators, policymakers, and community leaders.
   - Example: Propose programs that incorporate storytelling and mentorship to uplift Black boys.

By embedding the Sankofa framework into these sections, (re) searchers ensure that their work transcends academic boundaries, contributing to the liberation, healing, and empowerment of Black boys and men. Through deliberate acts of (re)membering, honoring lived experiences, and envisioning new possibilities, these expanded chapters demonstrate how writing becomes an act of divine creation and cultural restoration.

## CONCLUSION

As we conclude this chapter, we are reminded that writing divine words is not simply an academic endeavor but a sacred act—a calling to co-create with the ancestors, the community, and the divine. The Sankofa framework challenges us to engage in (re)search that is as much about healing and restoration as it is about inquiry. It compels us to look backward, to gather the fragments of wisdom left by those who came before us, and to forge them into a vision of a liberated future.

Through writing, we become freedom fighters, healers, griots, scientist that craft words that transcend the page and breathe life into the hearts and minds of Black people. Let us approach our work with intentionality, understanding that the power of the word lies not only in its intellectual rigor but also in its ability to inspire, mobilize, and heal. As (re)searchers, our responsibility is to create knowledge that uplifts and liberates, bridging the gap between academia and the lived realities of Black boys and men. The journey of writing divine words is both a privilege and a profound duty—an offering to our ancestors, a gift to our contemporaries, and a legacy for those who will follow.

May the words we write honor the interconnectedness of humanity, embody the spirit of Sankofa, and serve as a beacon of hope and transformation. May they inspire reflection, provoke action, and contribute to a world where liberation and justice are not merely aspirations but realities. Ase. Amen. Hallelujah.

# CONCLUDING SELF-REFLECTION EXERCISES

Part I: Self-Reflection

1. *Connecting With Your Purpose*

   • Reflect on your motivations for engaging in research on Black boys and men. Consider the following questions:

     o What experiences in your life have shaped your interest in this field?

     o How do your cultural background, identity, and positionality influence your approach to research?

     o In what ways does your research align with the principles of Sankofa—looking back to move forward?

Write a brief reflection (250–500 words) outlining your journey as a researcher and how your lived experiences inform your work. Consider how these reflections may shape your next steps.

2. *Invoking Ancestral Guidance*

   • Identify an ancestor or historical figure whose life or work resonates with the themes of your research.

   • Write a letter to this figure, sharing your intentions for your work and asking for their guidance and wisdom.

   • Reflect on what lessons or inspirations you can draw from their legacy.

Part II: Writing Preachable Words

1. *Testing the Power of Your Words*

   • Select a passage from your current research or writing that you feel embodies the spirit of divine words.

   • Read the passage aloud in a space where you feel comfortable and connected to your purpose.

     o Pay attention to how the words feel as you say them. Do they resonate? Do they move you emotionally or spiritually?

- Share the passage with a trusted colleague, friend, or
  mentor and ask them to read it aloud. Reflect on their
  reactions and whether the passage evokes the responses
  you intended.

2.  *Enhancing Preachability*
    - Rewrite the passage, focusing on the rhythm, cadence,
      and emotional resonance of the language. Incorporate
      metaphors, storytelling, or cultural imagery to make the
      passage more impactful.
    - Reflect on how these revisions align with the concept of
      writing as a sacred and transformative act.

Part III: Creating a Sacred Writing Practice

1.  *Designing Your Sacred Space*
    - Assess your current writing environment. Consider
      whether it reflects the intentionality and reverence
      needed for producing divine words.
      - What objects or symbols inspire and connect you
        to your purpose (e.g., photographs, candles, and
        spiritual texts)?
      - What rituals or practices could help you transition
        into a sacred state of writing (e.g., prayer, medita-
        tion, and lighting incense)?
    - Create or refine your writing space to honor its sacred
      nature. Document the changes you make and reflect on
      how they impact your writing process.

2.  *Integrating Rituals*
    - Choose one or two rituals to incorporate into your writ-
      ing routine. These could include the following:

- ○ Saying a prayer or affirmation before starting.
  - ○ Playing culturally resonant music or engaging in rhythmic movement.
  - ○ Invoking ancestors or offering libations.
- Practice these rituals for one week and journal about their impact on your focus, creativity, and sense of connection.

Part IV: Applying the Framework to Your (Re)search

3. *Revisiting Your Literature Review*
   - Reflect on the structure and content of your literature review. Consider the following:
     - ○ Are the voices of Black and African scholars adequately represented?
     - ○ Does your review honor the principle of (re)remembering, reclaiming suppressed narratives, and centering cultural authenticity?
   - Identify one area where your review could better align with the Sankofa framework and revise it accordingly. Write a brief reflection on the changes you made and their significance.

4. *Critiquing Your Methodology*
   - Review your research methods. Ask yourself:
     - ○ How do these methods honor the dignity and agency of your participants?
     - ○ Are your methods rooted in cultural authenticity and responsive to the spiritual, emotional, and communal dimensions of your research?
   - Propose one adjustment to your methodology that incorporates principles from the Sankofa framework (e.g., integrating rituals into data collection and engaging in co-creation with participants).

Part V: Visualizing Impact

1.  *Imagining the Future*
    - Write a brief narrative (250–500 words) envisioning the impact of your research on the lives of Black boys and men.
        - How will your work contribute to their liberation, healing, and empowerment?
        - What changes do you hope to inspire in communities, institutions, or systems?
    - Reflect on how the principles of the Sankofa (Re)search Model guide this vision.

2.  *Sharing Your Vision*
    - Create a presentation, poem, or spoken word piece that captures the essence of your research and its transformative potential.
    - Share this work with a trusted group or community and document their feedback.

Reflection Submission

Compile your responses, reflections, and revisions from the exercise into a document or journal. Use this as a resource to deepen your engagement with the Sankofa (Re)search Model and to guide your future work. By engaging with these exercises, you honor the sacred dimensions of your role as a (re)searcher, ensuring that your words and actions contribute to the *(Re)membering, (Re)storing, and (Re)birthing Black Boys and Men.*

# CHAPTER 6

## Final Thoughts: Our Process, the Future, and Who Can Be a Sankofic (Re)searcher

### AUTHORSHIP: EXPANDING THE WRITING PROCESS

A core component of Western thought that permeates the academy is the notion of rugged individualism. This cornerstone of Western philosophy and practice manifests in the academy through the authorship of scholarly writings, where single authorship is valued more highly than co-authored or collaborative efforts. Without delving into detail here—as we hope it is already evident to the reader—the Sankofa (Re)search Model aligns more closely with co-authored and collaborative approaches. Yet, while this book may appear to be co-authored, we contend that this is not entirely accurate, though we are still grappling with the appropriate terminology to describe our process. We did have lead writers for certain sections of the text and a lead organizer who led the process; however, for now, we would describe the book as having been *cyphered or co-cyphered.*

In hip-hop culture, the term cypher is briefly defined by the *Urban Dictionary* (2025) as two or more rappers or dancers engaging in a dynamic exchange, battling or playing off one another in a circle. However, Watkins and Caines (2014) offer a more dynamic description below:

> To cypher is to borrow and to lend, to playfully freewheel through whilst taking an exacting care for each word and carefully considering all the sounds, meanings, and interpretations. It is to fight back, to borrow, to steal, to represent, and to collaborate, whilst suddenly—surprisingly—at times aggressively claiming your own voice, your own right to speak. A cypher is a gathering of rappers, beatboxers, and/or breakers in a circle, extemporaneously making music together. (p. 1)

> In a cypher, one emcee will rap about a certain topic, which is quickly taken up or flipped by another emcee who plays off the prior words and themes. Each artist takes his or her respective turn, much like in a jazz solo. Cyphers flow freely between diverse performers who improvise their words, sounds, or movements to create a complex matrix of sharing. (p. 1)

As authors of the current text, we played off one another like musical improvisation, introducing thoughts, perspectives, and concepts into the circle of scholars through phone conversations, Zoom calls, text, and voice messages (the voice messages on texting platforms became one of our favorite and most useful spaces to cypher), and in-person meetings. Before entering or after exiting the circle of authors, we often had cyphers with our wives to try out new thoughts, much like a dancer experimenting with new moves in the mirror. When one of us received a *revelation*, we introduced it to the group, building on it and, in some cases, challenging ourselves to push further or even in a different direction.

Nevertheless, we first had to engage in "taking an exacting care for each word and carefully considering all the sounds, meanings, and interpretations." Yet, there was more to our cyphering approach that embodies the essence of the Sankofa (Re)search Model. In this model, cyphering is ritual.

Imani Johnson (2023) writes the following in the preface of her book on hip-hop cyphers: "*Dark Matter in Breaking Cyphers: The Life of Africanist Aesthetics in Global Hip Hop* focuses on the Africanist aesthetics of Hip Hop that are evident in its cypher rituals that ultimately hold together a global culture" (p. xii). She refers to the cypher as a ritual. Moreover, she positions cyphering as an ongoing manifestation of Afrikan practice when she writes that "Cyphering encapsulates an entire constellation of diasporic elements and sensibilities that Hip-Hop did not invent but rather rebirthed" (p. xiv). The ring shout (Rosenbaum, 2012), like the hip-hop cypher, was also a ritual of dancing and singing that took place in a circle among enslaved Afrikans in the Americas, with the explicit aim of channeling Divinities and Ancestors. Both these practices are predated by Afrikan religious practices such as the Akom of the Akan people of West Africa. The Akom also takes place in a circle, with counterclockwise dance movements accompanied by singing and drumming, with the goal of having the Abosom (Deities) and the Nsamanfo (Ancestors) appear or possess.

Taken altogether, we are saying that our work is not co-authored; instead, it was co-cyphered. We engaged in a circle, building ideas and concepts, playing off one another like jazz improvisation. Moreover, this process of authorship was a ritual. Our sacred circle did not consist solely of the three of us; we were joined by the Abosom, including the spirit of Sankofa, and the Nsamanfo. We offer this co-cyphering process as part of the Sankofa (Re)search Model.

We do not suggest single authorship; however, there are some cases, such as a dissertation, where you may not have a choice. In that case, you should still co-cypher. Create a group that you can build with and have reflective and critical dialogue. Develop the habit of picking your colleagues' and peers' brains about the things you are thinking about by asking, "What do you think about this or that?" Lastly, co-cypher with books and the Ancestors, as illustrated in McDougal's (2020b) *The Africology Imagination in Nocturne: Dreams of Sitting at the Table of Obaba: Unity, and the Come-Unity Line (Story One)*.

## GENERALIZABILITY OF THE SANKOFA (RE)SEARCH MODEL AND FUTURE WORK

Given our past theoretical work, we were asked to produce a research model for Black boys and men. While we have met this specific need, we contend that much of what we have produced is applicable to Black people in general. We encourage future scholars to use the existing model and apply it to other groups. We also call on researchers to expand on our work to make it more inclusive of all Afrikan people worldwide.

We make a special appeal to Black scholars trained in quantitative methods to reclaim quantitative approaches as Afrikan or Black pure thought and practice. This effort can help build a more robust and detailed Sankofic quantitative approach.

## WHO CAN BE A SANKOFIC (RE)SEARCHER?

There is some debate in Afrikan Traditional Religion (ATR) circles as to whether Deities like Ausar, Set, Heru, Oya, Oshun, and Ogun—just to name a few—truly exist as entities or if they represent forces of nature or energy. For the sake of addressing the question of who a Sankofic (re)searcher can be, we will proceed as if both perspectives are plausible—that these names represent both entities and energies.

Let us revisit the African trinity story of Ausar, Auset, and Heru. Auset plays the most significant role in the (re)membering of Ausar, as she searches—or (re)searches—for all Ausar's body members and eventually (re)births Ausar as Heru. If we see Auset as an energy, then anyone, male or female, can potentially possess the energy of Auset to (re)member and (re)birth Ausar and Heru. That is to say, anyone possessed by Auset's energy can possibly (re) search Black boys and men under the Sankofa (Re)search Model.

Auset is a female Afrikan Deity. If we see Auset as an entity in the form of a Black woman, then Black women are well-positioned to be part of the (re)membering, (re)birthing, (re)storing, cyphering, and (re)searching process. We argue that the Sankofa (Re)search Model functions best when Black women are part of the process, and there is no need for the field of Black Men Studies to be dominated by men.

Beyond the sentiments shared in the two paragraphs above, we are calling for a more structured and intentional approach by Afrikan scholars to prepare Sankofic (re)searchers. In Chapter 3, we asked you to think about your doctoral training, which can also be described as an initiation process that may even include what feels like hazing to many. For the most part, the current process for training PhDs in the social sciences, humanities, and significant aspects of physical sciences is an exercise in reading comprehension, writing, and reasoning. While these components are important, they fall woefully short of our contention that researchers must also be healers. Moreover, to be healers, researchers must also be trained to see and hear beyond their physical ears and eyes, like Dr. Carver and the priest who performed the hearing ceremony to determine the purpose of an unborn child, as described by Somé (2002).

We have noted that education and schooling are spiritual processes and transactions. This is why, in antiquity, healers and priests were in control of or responsible for pedagogy. The role of teacher— and, in this case, researcher—carries great weight, power, and responsibility, as both should be healers. Thus, Afrikan scholars need our own process for creating and initiating (re)searchers by drawing back on our indigenous systems and practices. We must broaden our expectations for our profession and craft.

To be a doctor, educator, and (re)searcher is to be likened to a priest. To fully answer the question of who can be a Sankofic (re) searcher, one must receive training and undergo initiation practices that mirror those taught and experienced in ancient and contemporary Afrikan indigenous systems (Assefa, 2016; Mahnzili, 2024). We must be dogmatically and indefatigably Sankofic, willing to (re)turn again and again, like Auset searching for fragments of our indigenous practices—not only to (Re) member, (Re)store, and (Re)birth Black boys and men but also to heal ourselves as (Re)searchers in the process.

## Postscript: *Confirmation*

We began and infused this work with prayers—a call for help and guidance from the invisible world—to create a work that would be healing for Black men, and boys in particular. The original manuscript was completed and submitted to the series editor. After reviewing it, he requested clarification on a couple of items concerning the exercises, which created the space for this addition and led to the following dream by the lead-cypherer.

> *Earlier that day, I had a long conversation with the series editor, during which we discussed, among other things, the potential impact of our work. Perhaps the conversation lingered in my mind as I drifted off to sleep that night. I found myself in a dream. There were about fifty Black boys—chocolate-skinned, with big smiles—joyfully playing on a playground. They appeared to be around 9, 10, or maybe 11 years old. Three boys approached me, sat on my lap, hugged me, smiled, and looked into my eyes. Then they said, "Thank you... thank you for your work. Thank you for all you do for us."*

> *I woke up immediately afterward, smiling, feeling profoundly blessed to have received such immediate and clear... confirmation.*

# THE SANKOFA (RE)SEARCHER OATH

*I am a Sankofic (Re)searcher of Black boys and men, which makes me a healer above all things. I do this healing work because I have an enduring and everlasting love of Afrikan people worldwide. In fact, Love is my introduction and background, Love is my goals and objectives, Love is my conceptual and theoretical frames, Love is my positionality,*

*Love is my (re)search questions and my hypothesis,*

*Love is my ontology, epistemology, and axiology, Love is my (re) search paradigm, approach, model, methodology, and method, Love is my analysis, codes, and themes, Love is my findings and results, Love is my discussion, recommendations, and conclusions. Because of Love, I commit to freeing myself and my work from reproducing deficit paradigms, colonized approaches, and plantation and caged scholarship as I thrive to*

*move from a space of pure, free, and decolonized Black thought.*

*Moreover, I am, and the (re)search I cypher, the mouthpiece of God. I am led by the Holy Ghosts and our Ancestors to write scripture, mdw ntr, and divine words. The spirit of Sankofa propels me on a relentless pursuit, to go back again and again, to (re)search and (re)search, for our knowledge, cultural ways, practice, rituals, and good ethics, which drives me to be like Auset finding fragmented pieces of our story and our bodies in order to (Re)member, (Re)store, and (Re)birth new Suns, new Herus, new Christs, or*

*new Black Boys and Men who reach their highest level of Divinity.*

*I willingly accept the responsibility and weight of my charge as a Sankofic (Re)searcher,*

*yet, I have no realistic alternative: My fate and entrance into a peaceful eternity are contingent on my ability to fulfill my commitment and oath.*

# *References*

Adams, J., Keane, W., & Dutton, M. (2005). *The politics of method in the human sciences: Positivism and its epistemological others.* Duke University Press.

African Creation Energy. (2010). *Supreme mathematic African Ma'at magic.* Lulu.com

Al-Ababneh, M. (2020). Linking ontology, epistemology and research methodology. *Science & Philosophy, 8*(1), 75–91.

Alim, H. S. (2006). *Roc the mic right: The language of hip hop culture.* Routledge.

Alim, H. S., Ibrahim, A., & Pennycook, A. (2009). *Global linguistic flows: Hip hop cultures, youth identities, and the politics of language.* Routledge.

Aliyu, A. A., Bello, M. U., Kasim, R., & Martin, D. (2014). Positivist and non-positivist paradigm in social science research: Conflicting paradigms or perfect partners. *Journal of Management and Sustainability, 4,* 79.

Amen, R. (2003). *Maat: The 11 laws of God.* Kamit Publications Inc.

American Psychological Association. (2020). *American Psychological Association* (7th ed.).

Anderson, J. (1988). *The education of Blacks in the South, 1860–1935.* University of North Carolina Press.

Anyiwo, N., Watkins, D. C., & Rowley, S. J. (2022). "They can't take away the light": Hip-Hop culture and Black youth's racial resistance. *Youth & Society, 54*(4), 611–634.

Arellano, L. (2022). Questioning the science: How quantitative methodologies perpetuate inequity in higher education. *Education Sciences, 12*(2), 116.

Areo, M. O., & Kalilu, R. O. R. (2013). Origin of and visual semiotics in Yoruba textile of Adire. *Arts and Design Studies, 12*, 22–34.

Asante, M. K. (1980/2003). *Afrocentricity: The theory of social change.* African American Images.

Asante, M. K. (1990). *Kemet, Afrocentricity and knowledge.* Africa World Press.

Asante, M. K., & Abarry, A. S. (1996). *African intellectual heritage: A Book of Sources.* Temple University Press.

Asante, M. K., & Mazama, A. (Eds.). (2005). *Encyclopedia of Black studies.* Sage Publications.

Asante, M. K., & Mazama, A. (Eds.). (2009). *Encyclopedia of African religion* (Vol. 1). Sage Publications.

Assefa, B. (2016). *A Century of magico-religious healing: The African, Ethiopian case, 1900–1980s.* The Red Sea Press.

Austen-Smith, D., & Fryer, R. G. Jr. (2005). An economic analysis of "acting White." *The Quarterly Journal of Economics, 120*(2), 551–583.

Baker-Fletcher, G. (1996). *Xodus: An African American male journey.* Augsburg Fortress Publishers.

Barnard, H. (2001). Surveying in Egypt. *System, 1*, 13.

Bangura, A. K. (2011). *African mathematics: From bones to computers.* University Press of America.

Barkhuizen, G., & Consoli, S. (2021). Pushing the edge in narrative inquiry. *System, 102*.

Bell, R. (1992). *Faces at the bottom of the well: The permanence of racism.* Basic Books.

Barnes, J. A. (2011). *Overcoming the odds: The success story of an African American gifted male student.* Electronic Theses & Dissertations, 554. http://digitalcommons.georgiasouthern.edu/etd/554.

Bonner, F. (2010). *Academically gifted African American male college students.* Praeger.

Brewster, A. (2022). *The healing power of storytelling: Using personal narrative to navigate illness, trauma, and loss.* North Atlantic Books.

Brod, H. (Ed.). (1987). *The making of masculinities.* Allan & Unwin.

Bronfenbrenner, U. (1979). *The ecology of human development: Experiments by nature and design.* Harvard University Press.

Bronfenbrenner, U. (1986). Ecology of the family as a context for human development: Research perspectives. *Developmental Psychology,* *22*(6), 723–742.

Bronfenbrenner, U. (1989). Ecological systems theory. In R. Vasta (Ed.), *Annals of child development* (Vol. 6, pp. 187–249). JAI Press.

Bronfenbrenner, U. (2005). *Making human beings human: Bioecological perspectives on human development.* Sage Publications.

Brown, A. L. (2011). Racialised subjectivities: A critical examination of ethnography on Black males in the USA, 1960s to early 2000s. *Ethnography and Education, 6*(1), 45–60.

Brown, A. L., & Donnor, J. K. (2011). Toward a new narrative on Black males, education, and public policy. *Race Ethnicity and Education, 14*(1), 17–32.

Bundles, A. L. (2002). *On her own ground: The life and times of Madam CJ Walker.* Scribner.

Bush, L. (1997). Independent Black institutions in America: A rejection of schooling, an opportunity for education. *Urban Education, 32,* 98–116.

Bush, L. (1999). Am I a man? A literature review engaging the sociohistorical dynamics of Black manhood in the United States. *Western Journal of Black Studies, 23,* 49–57.

Bush, L., & Bush, E. (2013a). "God bless the child who got his own": Toward a comprehensive theory for African American boys and men. *Western Journal of Black Studies, 37*(1), 1–13.

Bush, L., & Bush, E. (2013b). Introducing African American Male Theory (AAMT). *Journal of African American Males in Education, 4*(1), 1–1.

Bush, L., & Bush, E. (2018). A paradigm shift? Just because the lion is talking doesn't mean that he isn't still telling the hunter's story: African American Male Theory and the problematics of both deficit and nondeficit models. *Journal of African American Males in Education, 9*(1), 1–18.

Bush, L., Bush, E., & Causey-Bush, T. (2006). The collective unconscious: New thoughts on the existence of independent Black institutions. *The Journal of Pan African Studies, 1*(6), 48–66.

Bush, L., Bush, E., & Mahnzili, A. (2020). "Get Out!" Beyond the notion of "acting white": Schooling as spirit possession: Dismantling interpretations of African American student success. In P. Jones (Ed.), *Fostering Collaborations Between African American communities and educational institutions* (pp. 34–55). IGI Global.

Bush, L., Jeffers-Coly, P., Bush, E., & Lewis, L. (2022). "They are coming to get something": A qualitative study of African American male community college students' education abroad experience in Senegal, West Africa. *Frontiers: The Interdisciplinary Journal of Study Abroad, 34*(1) 257–279.

Byfield, C. (2008). The impact of religion on the educational achievement of Black boys: A UK and USA study. *British Journal of Sociology of Education, 29*(2), 189–199.

Cajete, G. (1994). *Look to the mountains: An ecology of Indigenous education.* Kivaki Press.

Cannon, K. (1988). *Black womanist ethics.* Scholars Press.

Castillo, W., & Babb, N. (2024). Transforming the future of quantitative educational research: A systematic review of enacting quantCrit. *Race Ethnicity and Education, 27*(1), 1–21.

Chaney, C., & Mincey, K. D. (2014). Typologies of Black male sensitivity in R&B and hip hop. *Journal of Hip Hop Studies, 1*(1), 121–156.

Clement of Alexandria. (2015). *Paedagogus: The instructor.* CreateSpace.

Cohen, L., Manion, L., & Morrison, K. (2002). *Research methods in education.* Routledge.

Collins, P. (1990). *Black feminist thought: Knowledge, consciousness, and the politics of empowerment* (vol. 2). Unwin Hyman.

Coleman, S. T., & Davis, J. (2020). Using asset-based pedagogy to facilitate STEM learning, engagement, and motivation for Black middle school boys. *Journal of African American Males in Education (JAAME), 11*(2), 76–94.

Connell, R. W. (1995). *Masculinities.* Allen & Unwin.

Cox Edmondson, V. (2009). A new business: Redirecting Black youth from the illegal economy. *Reclaiming Children and Youth, 18*(3), 16–20.

Crenshaw, K. W., Gotanda, N., Peller, G., & Thomas, K. (Eds.). (1995). *Critical race theory: The key writings that formed the movement.* New Press.

Creswell, J. W. (2009). *Research design: Qualitative, quantitative, and mixed methods approach* (3rd ed.). Sage.

Curry, T. J. (2017). *The man-not: Race, class, genre, and the dilemmas of Black manhood.* Temple University Press.

Delgado, R. (1995). *Critical race theory: The cutting edge.* Temple University.

Dixon, B. (2025, January 19). Our mission is personal. https://thehoneypot.co

Donnor, J. (2005). Towards an interest-convergence in the education of African-American football student athletes in major college sports. *Race Ethnicity and Education, 8*(1), 45–67.

Du Bois, W. E. B. (1909). *The Negro American family* (Reprinted 1970). The MIT Press.

Du Bois, W. E. B. (1969). *The souls of Black folk.* Fawcett World Library.

Du Bois, W. E. B. (2001). *The education of Black people: Ten critiques, 1906–1960.* NYU Press.

Du Bois, W. E. B. (2010). *The Philadelphia Negro.* Cosimo, Inc.

Duncan, C. (2010). *Cultural capital, habitus, and schemes: A case study of African American engagement in a secondary classroom* [Doctoral dissertation]. California State University, Los Angeles/University of California, Irvine.

Duncan, G. (2002). Beyond love: A critical race ethnography of the schooling of adolescent Black males. *Equity & Excellence in Education, 35*(2), 131–143.

Fenning, P., & Rose, J. (2007). Overrepresentation of African American students in exclusionary discipline: The role of school policy. *Urban Education, 42*(6), 536–559.

Folorunso, O., Akinwale, A. T., Vincent, R. O., & Olabenjo, B. (2010). A mobile-based knowledge management system for "Ifa": An African traditional oracle. *African Journal of Mathematics and Computer Science Research, 3*(7), 114–131.

Foote, M. Q., & Gau Bartell, T. (2011). Pathways to equity in mathematics education: How life experiences impact researcher positionality. *Educational Studies in Mathematics, 78*, 45–68.

Fordham, S. (1996). *Blacked out: Dilemmas of race, identity, and success at capital high.* University of Chicago Press.

Fordham, S., & Ogbu, J. (1986). Black students' school success: Coping with the burden of acting white. *Urban Review, 18,* 176–206.

Fortes, H. (1967). Kinship and marriage among the Ashanti. In A. Radcliffe-Brown & D. Forde (Eds.), *African systems of kinship and marriage* (pp. 252–284). Oxford University.

Franklin, C. (1984). *The changing definition of masculinity.* Plenum.

Franklin, C. (1994). Men's studies, the men's movement, and the study of Black masculinities: Further demystification of masculinities in America. In R. Majors & J. Gordon (Eds.), *The American Black male: His present status and future* (pp. 3–19). Nelson-Hall Publishers.

Freire, P. (1993). *Pedagogy of the oppressed.* The Continuum International Publishing Group Ltd.

Gbagbo, D. K., & Elder, D. R. (2019). Storytelling songs of the Èwè-Dòmè of Ghana. *African Music: Journal of the International Library of African Music, 11*(1), 91–112.

Gibbs, J. T. (1984). Black adolescents and youth: An endangered species. *American Journal of Orthopyschiatry, 54,* 8–20.

Gibbs, J. T. (1988). *Young, Black, and male in American: An endangered species.* Auburn House.

Goings, R. B. (2015). The lion tells his side of the (counter) story: A Black male educator's autoethnographic account. *Journal of African American Males in Education (JAAME), 6*(1), 91–105.

Goings, R. B. (2016). (Re) defining the narrative: High-achieving non-traditional Black male undergraduates at a Historically Black College and University. *Adult Education Quarterly, 66*(3), 237–253.

Gordon, E. T., Gordon, E. W., & Nembhard, J. G. (1994). Social science literature concerning African American men. *Journal of Negro Education, 63*(4), 508–531.

Gould, S. J. (1981). *Mismeasure of man.* W.W. Norton & company.

Grantham, T. C. (2004). Rocky Jones: Case study of a high-achieving Black male's motivation to participate in gifted classes. *Roeper Review, 26*(4), 208.

Grier, W., & Cobbs, P. (1968). *Black rage.* Basic Books, Inc. Publishers.

Grix, J. (2018). *The foundations of research.* Bloomsbury Publishing.

Guba, E. G., & Lincoln, Y. S. (1994). Competing paradigms in qualitative research. In N. K. Denzin & Y. S. Lincoln (Eds.), *Handbook of qualitative research, 2*(163–194), 105.

Guthrie, R, V. (1976). *Even the rat was white: A historical view of psychology*. HarperCollins.

Haddix, M. (2009). Black boys can write: Challenging dominant framings of African American adolescent males in literacy research. *Journal of Adolescent & Adult Literacy, 53*(4), 341–343.

Hammond, F., & Radical for Christ. (1995). We're blessed [Song]. *The Inner Court*. Sony Legacy.

Hare, N. (1971). The frustrated masculinity of Negro male. In R. Staples (Ed.), *The Black family*. Wadsworth Publishing Company.

Harper, S. R. (2010). An anti-deficit achievement framework for research on students of color in STEM. *New Directions for Institutional Research, 2010*(148), 63–74.

Harris, W., & Ferguson, R. (Eds). (2010). *What's up with the brothers? Essays and studies on African American masculinities*. Men's Studies Press.

Hersey, M. D. (2007). The transformation of George Washington Carver's environmental vision, 1896–1918. In J. L. Jordan, E. Pennick, W. A. Hill, & R. Zabawa (eds) *Land & power: Sustainable agriculture and African Americans* (pp. 57–76). Sustainable Agriculture Publications, Waldorf.

Herskovits, M. (1959). *The myth of the Negro past*. Beacon Press.

Hicks Tafari, D. N. (2018). "Whose world is this?": A composite counterstory of Black male elementary school teachers as hip-hop otherfathers. *The Urban Review, 50*(5), 795–817.

Hilliard, A. G. (1997). *SBA: The reawakening of the African mind*. Makare.

Hilliard, A. G. (2002). *African power: Affirming African indigenous socialization in the face of the culture wars: Commentary and selected bibliography*. Makare.

Holland, S. (1991). Positive role models for primary-grade Black inner-city males. *Equity and Excellence, 25*, 40–44.

Holling, C. S. (1973). Resilience and stability of ecological systems. *Annual Review of Ecology and Systematics, 4*, 1–23.

Holmes, A. G. D. (2020). Researcher positionality: A consideration of its influence and place in qualitative research—a new researcher guide. *Shanlax International Journal of Education, 8*(4), 1–10.

hooks, b. (1981). *Ain't I a woman: Black women and feminism*. South End Press.

hooks, b. (1990). *Yearning: Race, gender, and cultural politics*. South End Press.

hooks, b. (2000). *Where we stand: Class matters*. Routledge.

Howard, T. C. (2008). Who really cares? The disenfranchisement of African American males in PreK-12 schools: A critical race theory perspective. *Teachers College Record, 110*(5), 954–985.

Howard, T. C. (2013). How does it feel to be a problem? Black male students, schools, and learning in enhancing the knowledge base to disrupt deficit frameworks. *Review of Research in Education, 37*(1), 54–86.

Howard, T. C., & Flennaugh, T. (2011). Research concerns, cautions and considerations on Black males in a 'post-racial'society. *Race Ethnicity and Education, 14*(1), 105–120.

Hrabowski III, F. A., Maton, K. I., & Greif, G. L. (1998). *Beating the odds: Raising academically successful African American males*. Oxford University Press.

Hunter, A., & Davis, J. (1992). Constructing gender: An exploration of Afro-American men's conceptualization of manhood. *Gender and Society, 6*, 464–479.

Ikram, M., & Kenayathulla, H. B. (2022). Out of touch: Comparing and contrasting positivism and interpretivism in social science. *Asian Journal of Research in Education and Social Sciences, 4*(2), 39–49.

Jackson, A., & Sears, S. (1992). Implications of an Africentric worldview in reducing stress for African American women. *Journal of Counseling & Development, 71*(2), 184–190.

Jackson, R. (1997). Black "manhood" as xenophobe: An ontological exploration of the Hegelian dialectic. *Journal of Black Studies, 27*(6), 731–750.

Jeffers-Coly, P. (2022). *We got soul, we can heal: Overcoming racial trauma through leadership, community and resilience*. Toplight.

Jonathan, L. N., & Cinawendela, N. (2006). Problem child or problem context: An ecological approach to young Black males. *Reclaiming Children and Youth, 14*(4), 209–214.

Jones, M. K., Davis, S. M., & Gaskin-Cole, G. (2023). An integrative review of Sistah circles in empirical research. *Psychology of Women Quarterly, 47*(2), 159–179.

Jung, C. G. (1968). *Man and his symbols* (Reissue edition). Dell Publishing.

Junjie, M., & Yingxin, M. (2022). The discussions of positivism and interpretivism. *Global Academic Journal of Humanities and Social Sciences, 4*(1), 10–14.

Kaku, M. (2005). *Parallel worlds: A journey through creation, higher dimensions, and the future of the cosmos.* Doubleday.

Kaminer, D. (2006). Healing processes in trauma narratives: A review. *South African Journal of Psychology, 36*(3), 481–499.

Karenga, M. (1980). *Kawaida theory: An introductory outline.* Kawaida Publications.

Karenga, M. (1999). *Odu Ifá: The ethical teachings.* University of Sankore Press.

Karenga, M. (2004). *Maat, the moral idea in ancient Egypt: A study in classical African ethics.* Routledge.

Kenyatta, M. (1983). In defense of the Black family. *Monthly Review, 2,* 12–21.

Killam, L. (2013). *Research terminology simplified: Paradigms, axiology, ontology, epistemology and methodology.* Laura Killam.

Kim, J. (2011). Narrative inquiry into (re)imagining alternative schools: A case study of KevinGonzales. *International Journal of Qualitative Studies in Education, 24*(1), 77–96.

Kimmel, M. (Ed.). (1987). *Changing men.* Sage Publications, Inc.

Kimmel, M. (Ed.). (1995). *The politics of manhood: Profeminist men respond to the mythopoetic men's movement (and the mythopoetic leaders answer).* Temple University Press.

Kirkland, D., & Jackson, A. (2009). "We real cool": Toward a theory of Black masculine literacies. *Reading Research Quarterly, 44*(3), 278–297.

Kirton, O., & Rogers Jr, S. O. (2023). Aren't You the Valet? Tales of Black American Surgeons. *New England Journal of Medicine, 388*(9), e27.

Klatskin, M. (2018). Reclaiming the Black personhood: The power of the hip-hop narrative in mainstream rap. *Criterion: A Journal of Literary Criticism, 11*(1), 7.

Kremer, G. R. (Ed.). (2017). *George Washington Carver: In his own words.* University of Missouri Press.

Kumah-Abiwu, F. (2022). Urban education and academic success: The case of higher achieving Black males. *Urban Education, 57*(9), 1565–1591.

Kunjufu, J. (1985). *Countering the conspiracy to destroy Black boys* (Vol. I). African American Images.

Ladson-Billings, G., & Tate, W. (1995). Toward a critical race theory of education. *Teachers College Record, 97*(1), 47–68.

Lopez-Perry, C. (2023). Disrupting white hegemony: A critical shift toward empowering Black male youth through group work. *Journal of School-Based Counseling Policy and Evaluation, 5*(1), 21–25.

Love, B. L. (2016). Anti-Black state violence, classroom edition: The spirit murdering of Black children. *Journal of Curriculum and Pedagogy, 13*(1), 22–25.

Lynn, M. (2006). Race, culture, and the education of African Americans. *Educational Theory, 56*(1), 107–119.

Mackintosh, B. (1976). George Washington Carver: The making of a myth. *The Journal of Southern History, 42*(4), 507–528.

Madhubuti, H. (1990). *Black men: Obsolete, single, dangerous.* Third World Press.

Mahnzili, A. (2024). *Reshaping Black brilliance: Toward the development and implementation of a Pan-Afrikan pedagogy* [Doctoral dissertation] Claremont Graduate University.

Majors, R., & Billson, J.M. (1993). *Cool pose: The dilemmas of Black manhood in America.* Simon & Schuster.

Majors, R., & Gordon, J. (Eds.). (1994). *The American Black male: His present status and future.* Nelson-Hall Publishers.

Marfo, C., Opoku-Agyeman, K., & Nsiah, J. (2011). Symbols of communication: The case of Àdìǹkrá and other symbols of Akan. *Language, Society, and Culture, 32*, 63–71.

Maylor, U. (2009). "They do not relate to Black people like us": Black teachers as role models for Black pupils. *Journal of Education Policy, 24*(1), 1–21.

Marraccini, M. E., Lindsay, C. A., Griffin, D., Greene, M. J., Simmons, K. T., & Ingram, K. M. (2023). A trauma-and justice, equity, diversity, and inclusion (JEDI)-informed approach to suicide prevention in school: Black boys' lives matter. *School Psychology Review, 52*(3), 292–315.

Mazama, A. (2001). The Afrocentric paradigm: Contours and definitions. *Journal of Black Studies, 31*(4), 387–405.

McAdoo, H. (1988). *Black families* (2nd ed.). Sage Publications.

McCubbin, H., Thompson, E., Thompson, A., & Futrell, J. (Eds.). (1998). *Resiliency in African-American families*. Sage Publications, Inc.

McDougal, S. (2020a). *Black men's studies: Black Manhood and masculinities in the US Context*. Peter Lang.

McDougal, S. (2020b, April 4). The Africology imagination in nocturne: Dreams of sitting at the table of Obaba: Unity, and the come-unity line (Story one). www.afrometrics.org/decima/the-africological-imagination-in-nocturne-dreams-of-sitting-at-the-table-of-obaba

McDougal, S. (2017). *Research methods in Africana studies* (Rev. ed.). Peter Lang.

McMurry, L. O., & Edwards, L. M. (1981). *George Washington Carver: Scientist and symbol*. Oxford University Press.

Merriam, S. B. (1998). *Qualitative research and case study applications in education. Revised and Expanded from "Case Study Research in Education."*. Jossey-Bass Publishers.

Merriam, S. B., & Tisdell, E. J. (2015). *Qualitative research: A guide to design and implementation*. John Wiley & Sons.

Merriweather Hunn, L. R., Guy, T. C., & Mangliitz, E. (2006). Who can speak for whom? Using counter storytelling to challenge racial hegemony. *Adult Education Research 2006 Conference Proceedings*. KS State University.

Mills, Q. T. (2005). "I've got something to say": The public space, public discourse, and the barbershop. *Radical History Review, 93*, 192–199.

Mills Q. T. (2004). Truth and soul: Black talk in the barbershop. In M. Harris-Lacewell (Ed.), *Barbershops, Bibles, and BET: Everyday talk and Black political thought* (pp. 162–203). Princeton University Press.

Ming-Dao, D. (1986). *The wandering Taoist*. HarperCollins.

Moynihan, D. P. (1965). *The Negro family: The case for national action*. U.S. Department of Labor: Office of Planning and Research.

Morrell, E., & Duncan-Andrade, J. M. R. (2002). Promoting academic literacy with urban youth through engaging hip-hop culture. *The English Journal, 91*(6), 88–92.

Nobles, W. W. (1980). African philosophy: Foundations for the Black psychology. In R. Jones (Ed.), *Black psychology* (pp. 23–36). Harper & Row.

Nobles, W. W. (2023). *SKH: From Black psychology to the science of being.* Universal Write Publications LLC.

Noguera, P. A. (2003). The trouble with Black boys: The role and influence of environmental and cultural factors on the academic performance of African American males. *Urban Education, 38*(4), 431–459.

Nuryatno, M. A. (2003). The call for the paradigm shift in qualitative research from positivism and interpretive to critical theory. *Journal Hermeneia, 2*(1), 24–50.

Oamen, O. D. (2008). African storytelling: A dialectical construct. *Knowledge Review, 16*(4), 160–164.

Oamen, O. D. (2011). African storytelling and development. In D. Shober (Ed.), *Silencing the abusers: Death and marriage in African women's writing* (pp.185–195). Creative Commons.

Ogbu, J. U. (1987). Variability in minority school performance: A problem in search of an explanation. *Anthropology and Education Quarterly, 18*, 312–334.

Ogbu, J. U. (1991). Cultural diversity and school experience. In C. E. Walsh (Ed.), *Literacy as praxis: Culture, language, and pedagogy* (pp. 25–50). Ablex.

Okewande, O. T. (2020). African indigenous knowledge systems of mathematics and science: Insights from the faculties of Ifá among the Yorùbá of Nigeria. In A. Nhemachena (Ed.), *Decolonising science, technology, engineering and mathematics (STEM) in an age of technocolonialism: Recentring African indigenous knowledge and belief systems* (p. 151). Langaa RPCIG.

Opokuwaa, N. A. K. (2005). *Akan protocol: Remembering the traditions of our ancestors.* iUniverse.

Park, Y. S., Konge, L., & Artino Jr, A. R. (2020). The positivism paradigm of research. *Academic Medicine, 95*(5), 690–694.

Paulson, J. F. (2005). Surveying in ancient Egypt: From pharaohs to geoinformatics. *FIG Working Week 2005 and GSDI-8.* Cairo, Egypt. April 16–21.

Perillo, J. T., Sykes, R. B., Bennett, S. A., & Reardon, M. C. (2023). Examining the consequences of dehumanization and adultification in justification of police use of force against Black girls and boys. *Law and Human Behavior, 47*(1), 36.

Pino Gavidia, L. A., & Adu, J. (2022). Critical narrative inquiry: An examination of a methodological approach. *International Journal of Qualitative Methods, 21*, 1–5.

Pleck, J., & Pleck, E. (1980). *The American man*. Prentice-Hall.

Pleck, J. (1981). *The myth of masculinity*. MIT Press.

Poussaint, A. (1982, August). What every Black woman should know about a Black man. *Ebony*, pp. 36–40.

Ptahhotep, Hilliard, A. G., Williams, L. Obadele., & Damali, N. (1987). *The teachings of Ptahhotep: The oldest book in the world*. Blackwood Press.

Reynolds, R. (2010). "They think you're lazy," and other messages Black parents send their Black sons: An exploration of critical race theory in the examination of educational outcomes for Black males. *Journal of African American Males in Education, 1*, 144–163.

Richardson, E. B. (2006). *Hiphop literacies*. Routledge.

Rigaud, M. (1969). *Secrets of Voodoo* (Robert B. Cross, Trans.). Arco.

Roberts, G. (1994). Brother to brother: African American modes of relating among men. *Journal of Black Studies, 24*, 379–390.

Santrock, W. J. (2008). *Life-span development* (11th ed.). McGraw Hill.

Scotland, J. (2012). Exploring the philosophical underpinnings of research: Relating ontology and epistemology to the methodology and methods of the scientific, interpretive, and critical research paradigms. *English Language Teaching, 5*(9), 9–16.

Shabazz, D. L. (2016). Barbershops as cultural forums for African American males. *Journal of Black Studies, 47*(4), 295–312.

Simmons, K. (2025). *Art as medicine: Exploring the intersection of African cultural practices and art therapy to examine its efficacy in pain management and healing among Black women with Lupus* [Unpublished master's thesis]. Dominican University of California.

Singer, J. (2005). Understanding racism through the eyes of African American male student-athletes. *Race, Ethnicity & Education, 8*(4), 365–386.

Singh, A. (2003). *The hidden factor: An approach to resolving paradoxes of science, cosmology and universal reality*. AuthorHouse.

Skiba, R. (2002). *Special education and school discipline: A precarious balance. Behavioral Disorders, 27*(2), 81–97.

Smith, E., & Crozier, K. (1998). Ebonics is not Black English. *The Western Journal of Black Studies, 22*(2), 109–116.

Smith-Maddox, R., & Solórzano, D. G. (2002). Using critical race theory, Paulo Freire's problem-posing method, and case study research to confront race and racism in education. *Qualitative Inquiry, 8*, 66–84.

Solórzano, D., & Bernal, D. D. (2001). Examining transformational resistance through a critical race and Latcrit theory framework: Chicana and Chicano students in an urban context. *Urban Education 36*(3), 308–342.

Solorzano, D. G., & Yosso, T. J. (2002). Critical race methodology: Counter-story telling as an analytical framework for education. *Qualitative Inquiry, 8*(1), 23–44.

Somé, M. (1993). *Ritual: Power, healing, and community*. Swan and Raven.

Somé, M. (1994). *Of water and the spirit: Ritual, magic, and initiation in the life of an African shaman*. Penguin.

Somé, S. (2002). *The spirit of intimacy: Ancient African teachings in the ways of relationships*. HarperCollins.

Sonday, A., Ramugondo, E., & Kathard, H. (2020). Case study and narrative inquiry as merged methodologies: A critical narrative perspective. *International Journal of Qualitative Methods, 19*.

Soares, F., Johnson, R., & Davis, R. D. (2024). The Barbershop connection: A culturally relevant mental health approach to supporting Black men in college. In *Black Male College Students' Mental Health* (pp. 67–79). Routledge.

Spring, J. (2016). *Deculturalization and the struggle for equality: A brief history of the education of dominated cultures in the United States*. Routledge.

Staples, R. (1978). The myth of the impotent Black male. R. Staples, (Ed.). *The Black family* (pp. 98–104). Wadsworth Publishing Company, Inc.

Steele, C. M. (1997). A threat in the air: How stereotypes shape intellectual identity and performance. *American Psychologist, 52*(6), 613.

Steele, C. M. (1998). Stereotyping and its threat are real. *American Psychologist, 53*(6), 680–681.

Steele, C. M. (2011). *Whistling Vivaldi: How stereotypes affect us and what we can do.* W.W. Norton & Company.

Stevens, L. (2021). *Applying an anti-deficit based framework to aid in the cultivation of interest and entry into education, retention, and career advancement of Black male educators* [Doctoral dissertation]. Vanderbilt University.

Stinson, D. (2008). Negotiating sociocultural discourses: The counter story telling of academically (and mathematically) successful African American male students. *American Educational Research Journal, 45*(4), 975–1010.

Stinson, D. (2010). When the "burden of acting White" is not a burden: School success and African American male students. *Urban Review, 43*, 43–65.

Strain, T. H. (2023). *Zora Neale Hurston: Claiming a space* [Film Posse for American Experience]. PBS.

Sudarkasa, N. (1980). African and Afro-American family structure: A comparison. *The Black Scholar, 11*, 37–60.

Tatum, A. W. (2005). *Teaching reading to Black adolescent males: Closing the achievement gap.* Stenhouse.

Taub-Bynum, E. (1984). *The family unconscious: An invisible bond.* Theosophical Publishing House.

Toldson, I. A., & Owens, D. (2010). Editor's comment: "Acting Black": What Black kids think about being smart and other school-related experiences. *The Journal of Negro Education, 79*(2), 91–96.

Urban Dictionary. (2025, January). www.urbandictionary.com/define.php?term=Cipher

Uzun, K. (2016). Critical investigation of a qualitative research article from ontological and epistemological perspectives. *International Journal of Social Sciences and Education Research, 2*(3), 836–842.

Van Biljon, J., Renaud, K., & Chimbo, B. (2018, December). Visualization of African knowledge to embody the spirit of African storytelling: principles, practices and evaluation. In *Proceedings of the Second African Conference for Human Computer Interaction: Thriving Communities* (pp. 1–2). ACM.

Van Sertima, I. (Ed.) (1984). *Blacks in science: Ancient and modern.* Transaction Books.

Warren, C. A. (2021). *Urban preparation: Young Black men moving from Chicago's South Side to success in higher education.* Harvard Education Press.

Washington, A. R. (2018). Integrating hip-hop culture and rap music into social justice counseling with Black males. *Journal of Counseling & Development, 96*(1), 97–105.

Watkins, S., & McGowan, B. (2023). Exploring racism in the undergraduate and graduate school choices of scientists and engineers: Counterspaces for Black men. *International Journal of Qualitative Studies in Education, 36*(3), 356–368.

Watts, R. (1993). Community action through manhood development: A look at concepts and concerns from the front line. *American Journal of Community Psychology, 21*, 333–359.

Wells, K. (2011). *Narrative inquiry.* Oxford University Press, USA.

Welsing, F. C. (1974). The Cress theory of color-confrontation. *Black Scholar, 5*(8), 32–40.

White, J., & Cones, J. (1999). *Black man emerging: Facing the past and seizing a future in America.* W.H. Freeman and Company.

Whiting, G. (2009). Gifted Black males: Understanding and decreasing barriers to achievement and identity. *Roeper Review, 31*(4), 224–233.

Williams, P. (2009). *Exploring teachers' and Black male students' perceptions of intelligence* [Doctoral dissertation]. University of Miami.

Wilson, A. N. (1993). *The falsification of Afrikan consciousness: Eurocentric history, psychiatry, and the politics of white supremacy.* Afrikan World Infosystems.

Wilson, A. N. (1999). *Afrikan-centered consciousness versus the new world order: Garveyism in the age of globalism.* Afrikan World Infosystems.

Wilson, A. N. (2011). *Black-on-Black violence: The psychodynamics of Black self-annihilation in service of white domination.* Afrikan World Infosystems.

Wippold, G. M., Abshire, D. A., Wilson, D. K., Woods, T., Zarrett, N., & Griffith, D. M. (2024). Shop talk: A qualitative study to understand peer health-related communication among Black men at the barbershop. *Annals of Behavioral Medicine, 58*(7), 498–505.

Wood, J. L., & Turner, C (2011). Black males and the community college: Student perspectives on faculty and academic success.

*Community College Journal of Research and Practice, 35*(1), 135–151.

Woods, V. D., Montgomery, S., Herring, R. P., Gardner, R., & Stokols. D. (2006). Social ecological predictors of prostate-specific antigen blood test and digital rectal examination in Black American men. *Journal of the National Medical Association, 98*(4), 492–504.

Woodson, C. G. (1933/1990). *The miseducation of the Negro.* African World Press.

Wright, B. L. (2018). *The brilliance of Black boys: Cultivating school success in the early grades.* Teachers College Press.

Young, I. M. (1990). *Justice and the politics of difference.* Princeton University.

# About the Authors

**Nana Lawson Bush, V., PhD,** is the Chair of Pan-African Studies department at Cal State LA. Rooted in Pan-Africanism, Nana Dr. Bush employs a Pentecostal-revolutionary pedagogy—teaching from and to the spirit to foster a liberatory praxis. His approach to teaching is reflected in his research as he aims to contemporaneously disrupt power relations and to build programs, institutions, and states on the best of African philosophies and practices. He has published five books, including *The Plan: A Guide for Women Raising African American Boys from Conception to College* and *The Plan Workbook*, and 36 academic articles. Most notably, he published the first-ever comprehensive theory concerning Black boys and men called African American Male Theory (AAMT). Nana is a traditional Akan priest and healer. He is the father or baba of many children, but he has three biological children: two daughters—one medical doctor, one in medical school—and a son in his second year at Howard University.

**Dr. Edward C. Bush** is the President of Cosumnes River College in Sacramento, with a career in higher education since 1995 and extensive experience in the California Community College System. He holds a PhD in Urban Educational Leadership from Claremont Graduate University Dr. Bush is recognized for his innovative leadership, focusing on student success, equity, diversity, and access. Dr. Bush is a co-founder of A$^2$MEND, a nonprofit improving educational outcomes for men of color, and serves as the Chairperson for the All African Diaspora Educational Summit.

**Dr. Amiri Mahnzili** is an author and theorist whose work and research centers on a Pan-Afrikan theoretical approach to pedagogy. Obtaining his PhD from Claremont Graduate University in Cultural Studies with an emphasis on Africana Studies, Dr. Mahnzili's dissertation *Reshaping Black Brilliance: Toward the Development and Implementation of a Pan-Afrikan Pedagogy* explores a multitude of themes concerning the lived experiences of the Afrikan Diaspora including but not limited to Afrofuturism, Ante-Modernity, Anti-Colonial Movements, and precolonial Afrikan epistemology. Dr. Mahnzili also conducts Rites-of-Passage manhood training programs for young men throughout Southern California, which proved an instrumental resource for his theorizations for this text. Dr. Mahnzili's love and passion for Afrikan/Black people is exuded in his works and theorizations, his desire for Afrikan people to think beyond the confines and limitations of oppression and anti-Blackness to imagine a world and existence beyond these restricting ideations of the Black experience. Dr. Mahnzili is a loving father to his two children, Aynalem and Adonai, and a committed husband to his wife, Elilta.

*Sankofa (Re)search Model: (Re)membering, (Re)storing, and (Re)birthing Black Boys and Men*

Firmly grounded in theory and undergirded and informed by ongoing practice, this book is an important and thoughtfully developed contribution, not only to expanding the dialog and discourse of African American Male Theory, but also to Black Studies as a whole. The authors intentionally offer their work as an *invitation, invocation,* and *inquiry.* It is an invitation to collaboratively rethink how we do research in Black Male Studies to achieve healing, liberated and uplifting Black thought and practice in the interests of Black boys and men and the Black community. Questioning and crossing conceptual boundaries and frameworks, which they consider constricted, colonial and enslaving, they posit the invocation of spirit as both essential grounding and guidance for research and researcher. And they add right relationship with nature in the Carverian sense of love and listening as foundational.

Using the Akan concept of *sankofa* they pose inquiry as constantly reaching back, retrieving and reconstructing, building simultaneously also on the Osirian and Isisian narrative of (re) membering, (re)storing, and (re)birthing. To re-member is to constantly gather and reconstruct fragments of data of varied kinds to make Black boys and men whole again. To re-store is to resurrect, breathe new life into Black boys and men with the divine words and work that rightful research produces. And to re-birth is to use sankofa thought and practice to create and recreate methodological paths and paradigms for engaging and transforming Black boys and men and Black people as a whole in life-giving, life-enhancing, and culturally grounded ways. This work adds significantly to the continuously expanding scholarship in Black male studies and provides an engaging and valuable foundation and framework for African-centered ways of understanding and doing research.

# Index

Page numbers followed by "f" indicate figures; those followed by "t" indicate tables.